Bookkeeping using Excel

How to perform bookkeeping and financial reporting using Excel, only Excel, and nothing but Excel

Martin Mosfeldt, MBA

Copyright © 2012 Martin Mosfeldt

All rights reserved.

ISBN: 1477696156
ISBN-13: 978-1477696156

DEDICATION

To those readers that actually paid for this book: Thank you for your patronage. I sincerely hope you find it your money's worth, now as well as in years to come.

CONTENTS

	Acknowledgments	i
1	Introduction	1
2	Bookkeeping	11
3	Profit & Loss	17
4	Balance Sheet	23
5	Cash Flow	27
6	Explanatory Notes	37
7	Groups of Companies	41
8	Journal & Ledger	47
9	Errors	57
10	Exercises	65
11	Troubleshooting	73
12	Quick Reference	79

ACKNOWLEDGMENTS

Thanks to Philip Holst Riis, Ph.D. Fellow at Department of ITM, Copenhagen Business School for proofreading this book.

1 INTRODUCTION

Background

I hold a Master of Business Administration degree from Henley Business School, and I acquire, restructure and sell businesses for a living. My niche is in the low end of the market, where the costs of professional services need to be kept low for the deals to break even and make a profit. One of the reasons professional services costs tend to run up in this line of business, is because the paperwork has to be done not only for successful deals, but also for the ones that draw out. Another reason is that the legal and accounting work for a holding company with subsidiaries in dissimilar industries which change hands during a fiscal year is not simple.

Whenever I spin off or sell a new company, financial reports have to be made on that date. Many reports are needed in order to meet legal, tax, financing and buyer requirements. I do these reports myself, and have them countersigned by legally authorized professionals if necessary. Doing the reports myself benefits my business, because I understand better what is at stake, and because it allows me to test my ideas and calculate their consequences without incurring costs of outside assistance.

I could afford the initial cost of an advanced accounting package, but what I found I could not afford, was the cost of IT maintenance and learning-curve delays of professionals associated with such a package. To make an accounting package work for me, I would have had to put some effort into setting up accounts, financial reports, consolidated reports, tax calculations and so on, which in and of itself would perhaps not be a problem. Trading in companies is risky business however, and stakeholders will not commit capital if their exact financial reporting requirements are not accurately and convincingly matched. I found myself resorting to Excel anyway, in order to meet stakeholder requirements, and this gave me the idea to try and do the whole accounting system with Excel alone. If nothing else, at least it would save me the work of extracting and updating numbers from an accounting package, and it would also save me both the people work and the IT work of caring for such a package.

To keep costs down and flexibility up, I developed methods and routines to do the entire bookkeeping and reporting for all my companies and their holding company using Excel. Journal, ledger, profit & loss, balance sheet, cash flow, explanatory notes, VAT, rolling budget, fixed budget and consolidated group reports are documented and explained in this book, for you to use. Developing the system took several years. The version you are being given in this book is the fourth one, which, compared to the earlier ones, is a minimalist design. Anything and everything is centered about one thing and one thing only: keeping it simple.

The earlier versions had more automation and used more features of Excel, but time and again I found myself preoccupied with the sales and tax aspects of a new deal, enough so that I quite frankly could not remember how my Excel system worked. Also, once engulfed in the running of my business, I could ill afford the time to figure out how a complicated Excel spreadsheet worked. So I made it simpler until it was cut down to the bare essentials. If your time is as valuable to you as mine is to me, I suggest you, at least for a start, copy my instructions instead of developing new features and functions, tempting as such a creative endeavor might appear.

The basic financial reporting is covered in the chapters about bookkeeping, profit & loss, balance sheet, cash flow and explanatory notes. If you have some Excel proficiency and elementary accounting skills, I expect setting up your system for basic accounting will take you hours, not days, irrespective of whether you are starting from scratch or converting from an accounting package. If your jurisdiction has VAT, you will appreciate the consolidated VAT report in the chapter about groups of companies on page 41. To check out how the formulas work, have a look at the practice problem in the exercise chapter on page 65.

I hope you will be as happy with this solution as I am. For me, the decision to go with Excel has meant that I can match any reporting requirements including my own quickly and at very little cost, and that I am completely in control of the technicalities and IT issues that might otherwise create confusion.

Formalities

This text is written for an international audience using the English language, and language conventions differ around the world. My chosen convention for addressing people works like this: I reserve "you" for the purpose of addressing you, the reader, directly. About myself, I use the form

"I" rather than "we", because I am not a team. For a third person of unspecified gender I write "he or she". To reference you, me or a third person indiscriminately, I use "one".

Just to avoid any misunderstanding: By "Excel" I mean the spreadsheet program that comes with Microsoft Office. I use "the system" and "a system" about computers that run bookkeeping and Excel as defined here.

Some locales use period as the decimal mark, as in $\pi \approx 3.1416$. Other locales use comma, as in $\pi \approx 3,1416$. In this text, I use period as the decimal mark. If you use comma as the decimal mark, replace periods with commas in numbers if you copy/paste from this book.

The choice of decimal mark affects the choice of separator in Excel multi-operand function calls. In this text, I use comma as the separator in Excel multi-operand function calls. If you use comma as the decimal mark, replace commas with semicolons in multi-operand function-calls if you copy/paste formulas from this book.

The choice of decimal mark also affects the choice of thousands separator. In this text, I use comma for thousands separator.

Getting started

I assume you are building a system of your own. For that you will need a working Excel platform that supports ctrl-shift-enter SUMIFS, conditional formatting and data validation. It worked for me on both Excel 2007 and 2010 on a Microsoft Windows 7 platform. You can use the chapter with Exercises on page 65 to verify that your Excel version has what it takes, specifically the array implementation of SUMIFS.

I would suggest you develop your system as you go along, i.e. start bookkeeping based on whatever transactions are recorded on your bank statement right now, add accounts as you need them, and add report lines to your financial reports when you need them. It is quite unnecessary that you test your initial resolve and motivation by starting out with the massive chore of defining all the accounts you will ever need and all the report lines required by all stakeholders. On the contrary, I would suggest developing the system one step at a time is better, because one can see the results of one's work as it progresses.

A benefit of Excel is, that one can add formulas, columns and rows as one goes along. In this respect, Excel has been tried and tested by millions of imaginative and inventive users, in ways and with data I could not even begin to fathom. With Excel, changing accounts, report lines and formulas on the fly is easy. One need not be concerned Excel will fail just because of radical, extensive changes to rows and columns. Therefore I suggest you can safely assume, that whatever requirements the future will bring, you can still add solutions to your bookkeeping system when that time comes and trust Excel to grow with the task.

The chapters of this book are structured to support on-the-fly development. If you read the book from beginning to end and develop your own system along with your reading, the formulas and principles introduced in each chapter should make themselves apparent at suitable times.

A real world bookkeeping system must cope with the various forms of sales tax found around the world. These taxes differ, both in principle and in rate. I have included examples of how to do a single rate 25 % Value Added Tax (VAT), but I would suggest you set up your system without VAT first, and then work out your local sales tax formula on top of a working system.

Design

Bookkeeping is about economic and financial reporting, but it is also about managing massive amounts of numbers over time. Without exaggerating the risk, there is a genuine concern when using a system as flexible as Excel for bookkeeping, that the flexibility will lure the user into the woods, meaning a situation where there are sheets, formulas, numbers, transactions and formats all over the place, causing the user to lose self-confidence and the ability to systematically and consistently keep the bookkeeping up to date and free from errors. The design introduced in this book is meticulously crafted to manage this risk by keeping things simple. Because of the way the system is structured, the human task of keeping numbers in their right place becomes manageable.

When maintaining bookkeeping records in this system, one works with a "flat" file, i.e. a dataset with no superimposed database structure. When the system calculates report lines, the formulas operate directly on this flat file. The only function calls involved are SUM and SUMIFS. A write-protected copy of the flat file qualifies as a bookkeeping journal.

The way SUMIFS is used is admittedly somewhat advanced, but there is a chapter with exercises on page 65 where one can familiarize oneself with it. In my experience, when it comes to keeping ICT systems manageable, one is better off with a few, powerful functions that one understands really well, than with a lot of functions that one does not understand nearly as well.

One of the critical success factors for the design of the system is to keep complexity low. In light of this requirement, designing the whole account aggregation with just two function calls, namely SUM and SUMIFS, represents a design victory.

When working with the financial reports, i.e. Profit & Loss, Balance Sheet, Cash Flow and Explanatory Notes, there is no formula work involved in allocating accounts to report lines. The allocation of accounts to report lines is separate from the formulas, and done by putting a sub-list of accounts besides their report line. This separation of formulas and accounts is implemented by the somewhat advanced use of SUMIFS, where the function call refers to a separate array of accounts, specifically the aforementioned sub-list.

In the financial reports, the same formula is used for all the report lines. The individual customization of report lines is done with a sub-list of accounts, separate from the formula. By keeping the sub-list of accounts that belong in a particular report line separate from the formula that calculates that report line, one is free to move accounts between report lines without having to worry about getting the formulas right. This represents a design victory in relation to the objective of staying clear of complexity.

There are other niceties in the design, niceties that keep things simple and manageable, and the system is in operation and works today on this author's businesses. Moving ahead however, I will let the design speak for itself instead of painstakingly boasting each finesse.

Reference Model

As illustrated by the reference model shown on the next page, the system copes with multiple companies using the same list of account numbers for all of them, but with a separate file with bookkeeping records and a separate set of financial reports with report lines for each. Using different account numbers for the same thing depending on which company's books is being kept would make bookkeeping harder for the bookkeeper and interpretation of the financial reports harder for the stakeholders. A system with only a single company will have three spreadsheets in the workbook. The three sheets are referenced in this model as "accounts", "transactions" and "reports" respectively.

The relationship between the accounts sheet and the two other sheets is unidirectional. The accounts sheet is the master, the two other sheets use only such account numbers as are defined by the master. Neither the transactions sheet nor the reports sheet can update the accounts sheet.

The relationship between the reports sheet and the transactions sheet is bidirectional. In the reports sheet, report lines are calculated using formulas that read bookkeeping records from the transactions sheet. In the transaction sheet, control formulas to support the bookkeeping are calculated from report lines found in the reports sheet, as shown in the adjacent illustration.

Checks and balances are implemented using conditional formatting, an Excel feature that changes the color of report lines and bookkeeping records to bright alarming red if something is wrong. Data validation is implemented using the Excel feature of the same name. It limits the values one can enter into a field to the list of accounts in the accounts sheet, and assists data entry by offering a drop-down menu with the permitted values.

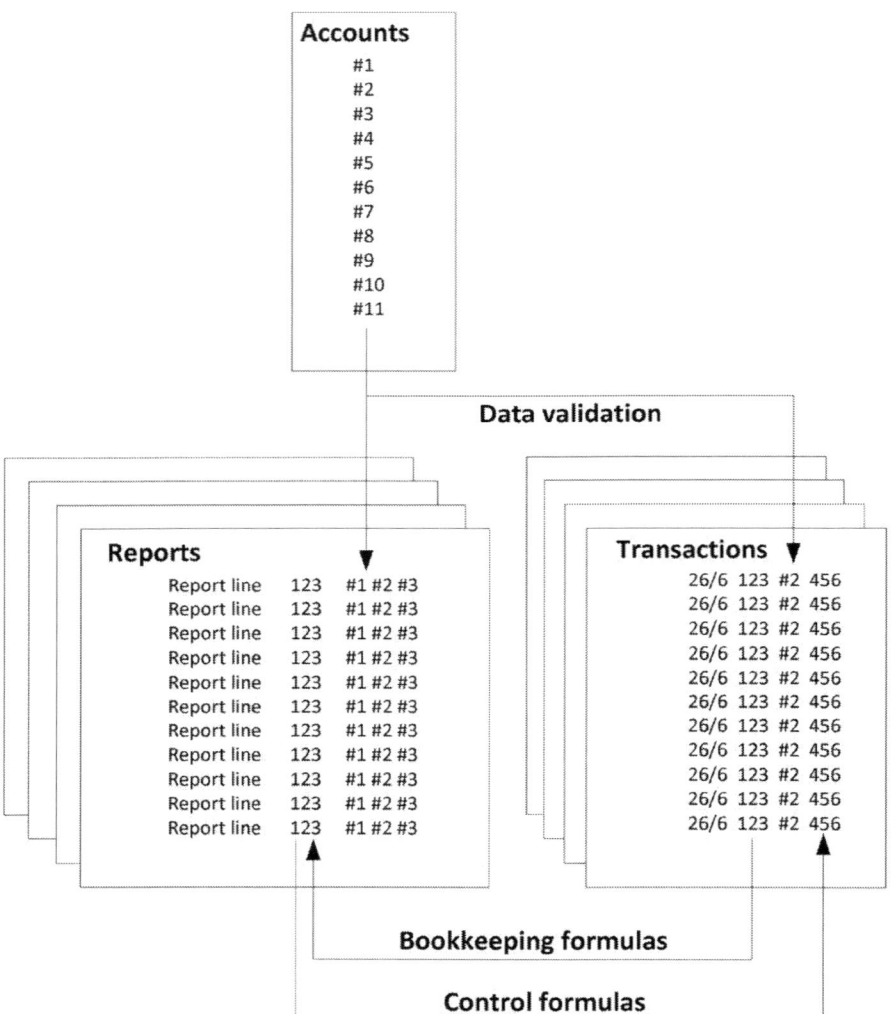

Bookkeeping formulas are constructed using arithmetic operators and the two built-in Excel functions SUM and SUMIFS. No VBA or other coding is involved in the bookkeeping formulas, so their maintenance does not require programming. Control formulas are entered on an ad-hoc basis. A control formula could for example be a calculation to determine a depreciation amount or a tax transferal. There can be as many control formulas as one likes, but there are only three bookkeeping formulas: One for the Profit &

Loss respectively for the Cash Flow report, one for the Balance Sheet report, and one for the Explanatory Notes report. The three bookkeeping formulas are static and do not change when report lines are added or modified.

Chapter Summary

- Develop your system as you go along
- Save VAT for round two
- Revere simplicity
- Three kinds of sheets: Accounts, transactions and reports
- Two kinds of formulas: Bookkeeping and control
- Two functions: SUM and SUMIFS
- Two features: Data validation and conditional formatting

2 BOOKKEEPING

Bank Interface

The bookkeeping records from a bank account statement could initially look like this:

	C	D	E
6	17-01-2012	Masonry Ltd	-351
7	19-03-2012	Masonry Ltd	-329
8	30-03-2012	Plumbing Inc	-2,500
9	17-04-2012	Loan	80,000

The meaning of these four records is, that on the date indicated, a transaction of the indicated amount was conducted. The descriptive text is often simply the name of the party with which the exchange took place.

Most of the records will be downloaded from the company's Internet web bank, which the company uses to pay and receive money. The download from the bank could be in the form of a comma-separated file or XML. Both of these download formats can be opened directly with Excel, so one can choose whichever one likes the better.

If the company's bank insists on using a dot-decimal format for dates, one can change the dots to dashes using Excel's Find/Replace function, which performs the change in one go on whatever spreadsheet area is selected, in this case an entire column.

The date format shown here is a European one, but the choice of date format has no bearing on the way the system works, because Excel stores dates as the same kind of integer numbers no matter what format one chooses to display them in.

The download from the bank contain more columns than the three shown here, but all the other columns are deleted. Earlier on I tried keeping the bank balance column for verification and auditing purposes, but I found out, that more general verification and auditing controls are necessary anyway, thus making a specialized bank balance control irrelevant.

Accounting

The bookkeeping work consists of assigning accounts and document numbers to transactions. The document numbers refer to the physical or computer-stored documentation that supports the bookkeeping record, typically kept in a set of physical binders where each document has a number written on it with blue ink or another permanent method.

The accounts are listed in a separate sheet that looks like this:

	A
1	0810 Services
2	0830 Energy
3	0840 Rolling budget
4	2112 Loan to Company 1

Even though it looks like two columns, this is in fact just one column. The account numbers and the account descriptive text is just one text field. I tried having them in two columns, but it added complexity and didn't really contribute any benefit. With accounts and document numbers assigned to bookkeeping records, the bookkeeping records could look like this:

	B	C	D	E	F	G
6	1	17-01-2012	Masonry Ltd	-351		0810 Services
7	2	17-02-2012	Masonry Ltd	-348		0810 Services
8	5	30-03-2012	Plumbing Inc	-2,500		0810 Services
9		17-04-2012	Loan	80,000		2112 Loan to Company

The document numbers are assigned consecutively to documents as they are put into their binders, and referenced in the bookkeeping records so one can always find the documentation to support the bookkeeping. This routine of remembering to put some documentation in the binders whenever there is a transaction I find has served me well. In my younger days, I used to believe I could easily recall whenever I had used my company credit card, only later to find out that I could remember neither why nor where I had put the documentation, if any.

To simplify the entering of accounts, the "Data Validation" feature of Excel is used. Under data validation is specified that the field contains elements from a list, namely the list of accounts in the accounts sheet. Tick "Ignore blank" and "In-cell drop-down" and specify the list using array notation, i.e.

=accounts!A:A

Doing it this way entails several advantages. First, Excel automatically presents a drop-down menu to select the account from, thus limiting the users choices to those accounts that are previously defined, which in turn ensures that mistyped accounts do not erroneously find their way into the bookkeeping. Second, the use of array notation ensures that as many accounts as one likes can be defined without hitting any hard limit. Third, data entry is faster, because one can select from a list instead of typing. Fourth, if a new account is needed, one can just add it to the accounts list on the fly, and have it present in the drop-down menu instantaneously. Fifth, one can copy/paste account numbers from other bookkeeping records if, say, a list of transactions all should be charged to the same account.

Automatic Accounts

In addition to what has already been explained, the bookkeeping records have two fields to record whether the transactions should incur Value Added Tax (VAT) and whether they are bank transactions, columns **A** and **F** in the illustration below.. The two fields have Excel data validation so that they may only be empty or contain an "I" or an "O" and a "B" respectively (for **I**ncoming VAT, **O**utgoing VAT and **B**ank). The significance of a "B" in the Bank field or an "I" or "O" in the VAT field is, that all such records are summed up in special automatic accounts that sit as bookkeeping records in the first lines of the transactions sheet, as shown below:

	A	B	C	D	E	F	G
1			31-12-2012	Automatic	-2,500		9011 Budget VAT
2			29-06-2012	Automatic			9010 Current VAT
3			31-12-2012	Automatic	-166,560		9003 Bank debt
4			29-06-2012	Automatic	89,761		9002 Bank debt
5			01-01-2012	Automatic	-166,560	B	9001 Bank debt
6		1	17-01-2012	Masonry Ltd	-351	B	0810 Services
7		2	17-02-2012	Masonry Ltd	-348	B	0810 Services
8	I	5	30-03-2012	Plumbing Inc	-2,500	B	0810 Services
9			17-04-2012	Loan	80,000	B	2112 Loan to Co

The automatic account, "9010 Current VAT", is calculated like this:

=0.2*SUMIFS(G:G,A:A,"I",C:C,"<"&TODAY())+
0.2*SUMIFS(G:G,A:A,"O",C:C,"<"&TODAY())

The automatic account, "9011 Budget VAT", is calculated like this:

=0.2*SUMIFS(G:G,A:A,"I",C:C,">="&TODAY())+
0.2*SUMIFS(G:G,A:A,"O",C:C,">="&TODAY())

The 0.2 reflects the current Danish VAT rate of 25 %, the G:G is the columns with transaction amounts, and the A:A is the column in which the "I" and the "O" are found. The date in cell C2 is calculated as follows:

=TODAY()-1

The formula calculates the VAT for all bookkeeping records in the bookkeeping sheet up until today. There are several advantages to maintaining automatic accounts in this way: Having the automatic accounts masquerading as regular bookkeeping records with their own accounts means, that subsequent financial reporting and auditing automatically includes the automatic accounts. Also, Excel lets you freeze the top lines of a sheet so that you can keep track of your automatic accounts while doing your bookkeeping.

Notice the dates on the three bank automatic accounts 9001, 9002 and 9003. The automatic account "9001 Bank debt" is the initial bank account balance for that fiscal year (a literal number). This initial bank account balance is necessary as otherwise the other Bank automatic accounts would not show the correct amounts. The automatic account, "9002 Bank debt", is calculated like this:

=-SUMIFS(E:E,F:F,"B",C:C,"<"&TODAY())

The "9003 Bank debt" automatic account is calculated like this:

=-SUMIFS(E:E,F:F,"B",C:C,">="&TODAY())

F:F is the column in which are found the "B". Notice the negative sign. Assets are recorded with a negative sign. Therefore, the sum of assets and liabilities including equity is zero. In my experience, corporate finance specialists seem to find this perfectly logical, whereas accountants seem to find it strange. I have chosen to do it this way, because it makes the formulas and the Excel spreadsheet simpler and faster to work with.

Accounting Rules

This concludes the chapter on bookkeeping as far as Excel is concerned. To do the actual bookkeeping though, certain things must be understood. For example, one can easily enter non-banking transactions with or without VAT, simply by writing them into the sheet. However, when non-banking transactions are entered, one must balance credit and debit manually. Also, when recording transactions that incur VAT, one must remember to specify "I" or "O" in the proper field.

If a depreciation of some asset in the balance sheet is entered, a corresponding cost must be entered into the Profit & Loss for credit and debit to balance. The number that goes into the P&L will be negative, the number that goes into the Asset account will be positive. The reason one does not have to balance credit and debit manually for bank transactions, is because the bank automatic accounts do this automatically. To verify that this principle of double-entry bookkeeping is maintained, the facilities described in the chapter about bookkeeping errors on page 57 apply.

One may be required to keep a journal, that is, a log of bookkeeping transactions for audit and control purposes, for example by taking quarterly write-protected copies of the transactions sheets and storing them in a safe place. If a general ledger is also required, one can easily be made by sorting the journal copy by account number and date.

Chapter Summary

- Web interface to Internet bank for download of bank transactions
- Bookkeeping record points to account and supporting document
- Automatic accounts for cash bank transactions and VAT
- Assets are represented by negative numbers
- Credit and debit balances in double-entry bookkeeping

3 PROFIT & LOSS

Report Lines

The income statement, the P&L, could look like this:

	A	B	C	D	E
1	P&L as of 21-06-2012	This year	Year to date	Last year	
2					
3	Revenue	0	0	20,000	
4	External cost	-9,337	-5,606	-3,892	0810 Services
5	**Gross profit**	**-9,337**	**-5,606**	**16,108**	
6	Salaries	0	0	0	
7	Depreciation	0	0	0	
8	**EBIT**	**-9,337**	**-5,606**	**16,108**	
9	Financial earnings	0	0	0	
10	Financial costs	-1,800	-600	-947	1300 Finance
11	**EBT**	**-11,137**	**-6,206**	**15,161**	
12	Tax	2,784	0	-3,791	1500 Corporate
13	**Earnings**	**-8,353**	**-6,206**	**11,370**	

The report lines are different for different companies, but there are some considerable standardization efforts going on. You may wish to have a look at the IFRS Illustrative Financial Statements in the publication "International Financial Reporting Standard for Small and Medium-sized Entities (IFRS for

SMEs)" which can be downloaded from the IFRS website, www.ifrs.org. In Denmark where my companies and I live, the authorities operate an Internet online system where I can enter my annual report manually, one report line at a time. The use of this system is mandatory, so I simply copied the report lines that are relevant to my businesses from that system. I heard the UK and the US have such systems too, and eventually all jurisdictions will have them, I suppose.

Time and again some stakeholder requires a report line different from the ones already there. To keep the P&L standardized, such requirements can conveniently be dealt with by way of 'explanatory notes', which I will get back to in a later chapter.

The column 'Last year' is taken from last year's annual report, which has been filed with the authorities. Since these numbers are static, there are no formulas or calculations involved in their making. The summation rows (e.g. Gross Profit, EBIT, EBT and Earnings) are calculated by summation, as for example in this year's EBT:

$$=SUM(B8:B10)$$

The columns 'This year' and 'Year to date' are where the bookkeeping records are summed up into reporting lines. The difference between these two columns is that 'Year to date' only counts records that have a date before today's, whereas 'This year' counts all records on file. After year end, the two columns will become identical.

Rolling Budget

The purpose of including transactions that have not occurred yet in the bookkeeping is to implement what is known as a "Rolling Budget". In the beginning of the year, a future transaction is recorded on the rolling budget account, equal to last year's external costs. Also, expected income, say receivable interest or sales projections, are recorded as future transactions. This provides a forecast of what the fiscal year will end up looking like.

As the year progresses, future transactions are brought up-to-date. When the future becomes the present, current transactions are updated with their factual amount, and the remaining future transactions are reviewed and revised, so the rolling budget gradually becomes more and more accurate, and so financial dilemmas are recognized in good time.

One financial dilemma of particular prominence is the budget variation in relation to a fixed budget, if there is one. A fixed budget can be defined explicitly, for example because board or management negotiated it, or implicitly, for example because of financial projections released to investors. To monitor budget variation in relation to a fixed budget during the course of the fiscal year, one could have a "Fixed Budget" column with static numbers to the left of the "This year" column. The difference between the rolling budget and the fixed budget then becomes the budget variance, for management to act upon with hiring freezes, investment stops, budget cuts and so on.

Another important financial dilemma is budget variation in relation to available cash reserves, but for a wholly owned group of companies it is the consolidated cash position that limits the group's financial headroom, and therefore this will be discussed in the chapter about groups of companies on page 41.

Formulas

The formulas used to calculate 'This year' and 'Year to date' will require some considerable explaining. In row number 3, the "Revenue" report line in the above P&L example, they look like this:

{=SUM(0.8*SUMIFS(transactions!$E:$E,transactions!$G:$G,$E3:$Y3)+0.2*SUMIFS(transactions!$E:$E,transactions!$A:$A,"",transactions!$G:$G,$E3:$Y3))}

{=SUM(0.8*SUMIFS(transactions!$E:$E,transactions!$E:$E,"<"&TODAY(),transactions!$G:$G,$E3:$Y3)+0.2*SUMIFS(transactions!$E:$E,transactions!$C:$C,"<"&TODAY(),transactions!$A:$A,"",transactions!$G:$G,$E3:$Y3))}

To justify these formulas, I will need to explain not only how they work, but also why they represent good design. There are as many ways to set up Excel formulas as there are users, millions of different ways, and the fact that one of them works is not in and of itself enough to justify one over another.

From an IT technical perspective, this design is stateless in the sense that there are no intermediate stored data. This is an attractive quality, because it means transactions are reflected immediately in the report. The formula could be made to appear simpler by storing intermediate results elsewhere in the sheets, but these intermediate stored results would represent a potential source of errors.

Consider for example what happens if a new report line is added. If the formulas were dependent on intermediate stored data elsewhere in the sheet, it would be necessary to add a new line of intermediate stored data elsewhere in the sheet too. Using the formulas as they are coded here, that is, without intermediate stored data, the formulas operate directly on the bookkeeping records in the 'transactions' sheet. Since there are no intermediate stored data, the resulting P&L report reflects the recorded transactions directly and instantaneously.

The design uses the built-in Excel functions SUM and SUMIFS. These functions are, in my experience, fast and reliable. The formulas are coded using matrix array notation, e.g. $E:$E. This means there is no hard limit to the number of transactions the system can handle, which again is an attractive quality, because it means such hard limits do not have to be maintained manually as the numbers of accounts, bookkeeping records and companies grow.

Vectors

Turning from design to the question of how it works, consider this part of the formulas:

SUMIFS(transactions!$E:$E,transactions!$G:$G,$E3:$Y3)

The expression sums the E column in the "transaction" sheet if the G column matches one of the accounts in row 3. Besides each report line in the P&L, there is up to twenty-one accounts to be aggregated into that report line. The SUMIFS does this and returns an array, also known as a vector, with 21 elements, because the entire expression is entered as a vector formula, which is what the curly braces signify. In Excel, to enter a vector formula, the formula is written as one normally would, whereupon Ctrl-shift-enter is pressed.

The SUM aggregates the vector elements into one number. The reason the vector appears twice in the sum, once multiplied with 0.2 and once multiplied with 0.8, is to get the VAT right. The logic of this is, that VAT is deducted from all transactions, and then added back again to those transactions that should not incur VAT, identifiable because their A column is empty, i.e. contains "". The expression for the "Year to date" column is the same as the "This year" column, except for the clause that picks out transactions that have a date prior to today.

The choice of twenty-one as the right maximum number of accounts to aggregate into each report line is arbitrary. Initially I had ten, but then one of my companies needed eleven, so I upped the number. The fields in which the 21 accounts go, the $E3:$Y3, all have data validation using the list of accounts in the accounts sheet which means, that accounts can be reallocated to other reporting lines quickly and without typing errors.

The formulas for the "Revenue" report line can be copy/pasted to all the other P&L report lines that are not sums. The sums are the ones printed in bold in the P&L example, i.e. Gross profit, EBIT, EBT and Earnings. For completeness, I mention that the $ signs freeze columns when copying formulas around in the spreadsheet, useful when copying from the "this year" column to the "year-to-date" column.

Performance

The design choices made in this system reads as a catalogue of things that can cause performance problems in Excel. The idea behind this is to keep things manageable by sacrificing machine performance in favor of simplicity. Excel was not invented for bookkeeping, so additional design principles over and above Excel's own are needed for bookkeeping to be stable and reliable.

I use a good-quality laptop I bought in 2010, which seems to be OK up to about one thousand bookkeeping records. If you wish, you can test the performance limit of your hardware by adding dummy transactions to your transactions sheet until performance is degraded. If you do this, I suggest you make a separate copy of your Excel workbook to experiment with. I do not recommend mixing experiments with production, because of the risk of finding experiment leftovers in the production system potentially forever.

I would suggest the performance limit of the hardware and the software is not the limiting factor, because there is also a human factor, namely the necessity of keeping things manageable. I prefer to aggregate selected records by month or type, filing an aggregation document in the document binders, rather than allowing one of my company's transactions file to grow to more than a thousand records.

If, for example, some company has a lot of retail cash-register and credit-card transactions, maintaining each one of these transactions as a separate bookkeeping record in Excel may easily lead to both computer performance and human interface issues. After all, if one's inclination is towards the freedom and flexibility of Excel, how exciting is it to labor away with endless, monotonous cash-register or credit-card transactions? I for one would prefer to make aggregate records for the week or the month, and give the aggregate records a separate document in the binder for that company. Incidentally, this may be good idea from a general accounting perspective too.

Another reason I believe a thousand records in my case is enough, is because I want to have the full feature set of Excel at my disposal when I trace accounting errors or do what-if calculations, without suffering a performance penalty. One should reserve the capability to add spontaneous, unplanned formulas when the situation calls for it. Also, the techniques detailed in the troubleshooting chapter on page 73 are easier to apply successfully if there are not too many bookkeeping records.

Chapter Summary

- Three report columns: This year, Year to date and Last year
- Rolling budget based on future transactions
- Optional fixed budget for budget variance follow-up
- Two bookkeeping formulas for P&L report lines
- Vector formulas operate directly on transactions
- Performance sacrificed in favor of simplicity
- Hardware dependent soft performance limit

4 BALANCE SHEET

Report Lines

The balance sheet could look like this:

	A	B	C	D	E	F	G
15	Balance as of 21-06-2012						
16	ASSETS	This year	Year to date	Last year			
17	Loans to the	2,784	0	5,400	2112		
18	Receivables	2,784	0	5,400			
19	Cash	78,204	83,535	89,761	9001	9002	9003
20	Working capital	80,988	83,535	95,161			
21	Total assets	80,988	83,535	95,161			
22							
23	LIABILITIES & EQUITY	This year	Year to date	Last year			
24	Taxes	3,371	3,371	3,791	9010	9011	3110
25	Short term debts	3,371	3,371	3,791			
26	Total debt	3,371	3,371	3,791			
27	Share capital	80,000	80,000	80,000			
28	Dividend	0	0	5,400	1803		
29	Retained	-2,383	-236	5,970			
30	Equity	77,617	79,764	91,370			
31	Liabilities/equity	80,988	83,135	95,161			

As in the P&L, the "Last year" column is taken from last year's annual report which has been filed with the authorities. Since these numbers are static, there are no formulas or calculations involved in their making.

Certain special report lines are calculated directly instead of via bookkeeping records. For example, in this particular example, the retained earnings for this year is last years retained earnings plus this year's loss (-2,383=5,970-8,353).

As mentioned in the discussion of automatic accounts that begins on page 13, assets are represented by negative numbers, which is unusual in accounting but customary in corporate finance. To make assets represented by negative numbers appear as positive numbers in the report, an Excel custom format is used. Consider for example the Asset report line "Cash", which aggregates the three automatic accounts 9001, 9002 and 9003, and which were discussed starting on page 13. The "Bank" report line will have the value -78204 by year end, a negative number which represents an asset, namely 78204 currency units on the company's bank account. This number shows up as a positive number in the financial report, because all the assets have a user defined custom format that present positive numbers with a minus sign in front and negative numbers without. The custom format looks like this:

$$-\#.\#\#0;\#.\#\#0$$

The use of a custom numeric format for assets represents a design choice, the merit of which hopefully will become apparent in later chapters.

Formulas

The formulas to calculate the "This year" and "Year to date" columns are the same as the formulas used in the P&L, except whatever is in the "Last year" columns must be added. The logic of this is, that assets, equity and liabilities accumulate over the years, so their balance when the year started must be added to whatever was earned during the year.

Take for example, the formula for "This year" of the reporting line "Taxes" which happens to be line 24 in this particular spreadsheet. It looks like this:

{=$D24+SUM(0.8*SUMIFS(transactions!$E:$E,transactions!$G:$G,$E24:$Y24)+0.2*SUMIFS(transactions!$E:$E,transactions!$A:$A,"",transactions!$G:$G,$E24:$Y24))}

The $D24+ in the beginning of the expression adds the number from the column "Last year", but that aside, the expression is the same as the one used in the P&L.

Housekeeping

Now that both the P&L and the balance sheet have been explained, it is time to have a closer look at the accounts list in the accounts sheet again. There can be as many accounts as one likes, and one can use as many of them as one likes. Ordinarily, therefore, after a while, most bookkeepers find themselves the proprietors of quite a long list of accounts, easily hundreds. This is not a problem, the list can have any length, but there are some housekeeping rules to follow. The housekeeping rules are explained here, a later chapter will describe how to discover housekeeping errors.

Of all the accounts in the list, some are used, some are not. Call the accounts that are in fact used the 'active set'. All the accounts in the active set must be present one, and only one, time besides either the P&L or the balance sheet. This is how bookkeeping records find their way into the financial report. For example, in the expression for Taxes used to illustrate the formulas in the balance sheet, the SUM.IFS looks for a match in the list of account number $E24:$Y24. If there is no match in any report line, the corresponding records will not be aggregated by any SUM.IFS, and money will be missing from the financial report.

One can have accounts that are not part of the active set present in the financial report. In the beginning of the year for example, all the revenue and external cost accounts are not yet active, but I let them stay in the financial report nevertheless, because I know they will become active after a while.

One cannot delete or modify an account from the active set directly, because it appears several places in the workbook. If an account in the active set needs to be modified, it must be modified everywhere it appears. This can conveniently be done with Find/Replace. If one chooses "Within: Workbook" and ticks off "Match case" and "Match entire cell contents" in the Replace Options, the account will be changed everywhere it appears. If an account in the active set needs to be deleted, it must first be inactivated by replacing it with some other account everywhere it appears. Again, this can conveniently be done with Find/Replace.

Another convenient facility when working with accounts is data filtering. When one activates data filtering on the column in the transaction sheet that contains the accounts, Excel presents a drop down menu from which one can tick off accounts to filter. Excel filters away everything but the accounts one ticks off.

Chapter Summary

- Retained earnings calculated from P&L and last year's balance
- Custom numeric reverse-sign format used for assets
- Two bookkeeping formulas for balance sheet report lines
- Active accounts are allocated to either P&L or balance sheet
- Find/replace used to modify active accounts

5 CASH FLOW

Report Lines

The cash flow could looks like this:

	A	B	C	D	E
		This year	Year to date		
54	**Cash flow as of 22-06-2012**				
55					
56	**Cash flow from operations**				
57	Earnings	-8,353	-5,806		
58	**Changes, balance sheet**				
59	Fall (rise) in trade receivables	0	0		
60	**Net cash flow from operation**	**-8,353**	**-5,806**		
61					
62	**Cash flow from financing**				
63	Borrowing (repayment), loans	2,616	5,400		2112
64	TAXES and VAT... ...continued	-420	-420		9010 9011 3120 3110
65	Dividends	-5,400	-5,400		1803
66	**Net cash flow from financing**	**-3,204**	**-420**		
67					
68	**Net cash increase (decrease)**	**-11,557**	**-6,226**		
69	Cash at start of year	89,761	89,761		9001
70	**Cash at end of year**	**78,203**	**83,535**		9002 9003

Notice the three automatic accounts 9001, 9002 and 9003 which together sum up to the overall cash flow directly. The "Cash at end of year" field has the custom format used for assets, which reverses the sign,

$$-\#.\#\#0;\#.\#\#0$$

The formula to calculate the cash flow report lines is the same as the formula for the P&L report lines, and the account numbers to put besides the report lines are the same ones that are found besides the balance sheet, that is, all the accounts excluding those account numbers that go into the P&L. The logic of this is, that any difference between earnings and cash flow must be reflected as a change in the balance sheet. The operational balance sheet accounts are put besides the 'cash flow from operations' report lines, and the financial balance sheet accounts besides the 'cash flow from financing' report lines. The summation lines in the cash flow report are calculated bottom up. Consider for example row 60 in the below table. It is calculated from row 66 and 68, who in turn is calculated from row 70, that is, "bottom-up".

	A	B	
54	**Cash flow as of 22-06-2012**	This year	
55			
56	**Cash flow from operations**		
57	Earnings	-8,353	=b68-sum(b58:b59)
58	**Changes in assets and liabilities**		
59	Fall (rise) in trade receivables	0	
60	**Net cash flow from operations**	-8,353	=b68-b66
61			
62	**Cash flow from financing**		
63	Borrowing (repayment) of loans	2,616	
64	TAXES and VAT	-420	
65	Dividends	-5,400	
66	**Net cash flow from financing**	-3,204	=sum(b62:b65)
67			
68	**Net cash increase (decrease)**	-11,557	=-b69-b70
69	Cash at start of year	89,761	
70	**Cash at end of year**	78,203	

Mathematically, when one has a set of positive and negative numbers that add up to zero and remove some of them, the sum of the ones removed will be numerically equal to the sum of the ones that are still there. It follows, that if one takes the P&L accounts out of a report, the remaining accounts will sum up to the earnings. This is an example of a benefit of recording assets as negative numbers. In this instance, the housekeeping related to the Cash Flow report becomes easy, because all one has to do is copy and rearrange the accounts from the balance sheet. Also, the formulas become the same for all the cash flow report lines.

A decrease in the amount of assets held by the company generates cash, an increase in the company's liabilities generates cash. Since assets are recorded as negative numbers, these two statements can be combined into one statement: A change in assets or liabilities generates an equivalent amount of cash. Therefore, the formula to calculate cash flow report lines must compute changes to balance sheet report lines, which is what the P&L formulas do when applied to balance sheet accounts. For good measure, the formulas without VAT applied to row 65, "Dividends", above are

{=SUM(SUMIFS(transactions!$E:$E,transactions!$G:$G,$E65:$Y65))}

{=SUM(SUMIFS(transactions!$E:$E,transactions!$E:$E,"<"&TODAY(),transactions!$G:$G,$E65:$Y65))}

With 25 % VAT they are

{=SUM(0.8*SUMIFS(transactions!$E:$E,transactions!$G:$G,$E65:$Y65)+0.2*SUMIFS(transactions!$E:$E,transactions!$A:$A,"",transactions!$G:$G,$E65:$Y65))}

{=SUM(0.8*SUMIFS(transactions!$E:$E,transactions!$E:$E,"<"&TODAY(),transactions!$G:$G,$E65:$Y65)+0.2*SUMIFS(transactions!$E:$E,transactions!$C:$C,"<"&TODAY(),transactions!$A:$A,"",transactions!$G:$G,$E65:$Y65))}

A benefit of calculating cash flow directly from bookkeeping records instead of from the P&L and the balance sheet is that one can calculate it indubitably without resorting to previous years financial reports.

The Cash Flow report itemizes where cash stems from, particularly whether cash stems from earnings or changes to assets, liabilities and equity. The Cash Flow may well be used to itemize the cash generation attributable to diverse asset classes such as for example different kinds of investors and different kinds of loans and leases. On the following pages is a larger more detailed example of the financial reports including P&L, balance sheet and cash flow. First is shown the accounts list, which conveniently fits in a single page of this paperback format. Second is shown the financial reports, who fit on two pages that face each other. Third is shown the account allocation, which also fits on two pages facing each other. Notice the meaning of the cash flow report lines. Business operation has generated a positive cash flow from negative earnings of 386,954 currency units (CU), essentially by selling off fixed assets worth 13,621,777 CU, but proceeds from the sale worth 7,966,288 CU are tied up as trade receivables, so only 5,269,853 CU of cash are generated by the sale. Another 882,291 CU are obtained by borrowing, but most of all that cash is returned to the company's investors in the form of a dividend worth 2,098,104 CU and a spin-off worth 3,692,729 CU, leaving 361,310 CU to be put in the company's bank account.

Accounts	Usage count
0110 Revenue from rental	24
0130 Agricultural support	3
0411 Profit on sale of land	1
0610 Attorney assistance	2
0611 Auditor assistance	1
0640 Land registration fee	1
0810 Services	21
0820 Materials	3
0830 Energy	14
0831 Water	3
0910 Salaries paid	5
0920 Contained withholding tax	5
0921 Pensions, maternity leave, etc.	5
1001 Depreciation of inventory	1
1110 Retained earnings	1
1210 Property tax	1
1220 Insurance	1
1300 Financial costs	10
1500 Tax on profit or loss	1
1803 Proposed dividends	1
2110 Debt notes	14
2114 Receivable from sale of land	1
2120 Bank guarantees and deposits	2
2200 stock	2
2410 Property and buildings	2
3110 VAT	4
3120 Corporate income tax	2
3510 Mortgage	1
3511 Repayment of debt	1
3520 Loan from company X	2
3522 Loan from company Y	6
9003 Budget impact, bank account	1
9002 Bank account, current balance	1
9001 Bank account, initial balance	1
9010 Incurred VAT	1
9011 Budget impact, VAT	1

Income statement as of 30-06-2012

	This year	Year to date
Revenue	372,051	157,337
External costs	-273,610	-250,802
Gross Profit	**98,441**	**-93,465**
Personnel Costs	-70,353	-70,353
Depreciation and amortization	-12,468	-12,468
Financial costs	-254,527	-210,668
Profit before tax	**-238,907**	**-386,954**
Taxes	59,727	
Profit	**-179,180**	**-386,954**

Disposition of earnings

Proposed dividends included in own funds	0	0
Reserve for net write-up on equity method	0	0
Transferred results	-179,180	-386,954
Total	**-179,180**	**-386,954**

Balance sheet as of 30-06-2012

ASSETS	This year	Year to date
Land and buildings	0	0
Tangible fixed assets, total		
Fixed assets total		
Manufactured goods and merchandise	0	0
Total in stock		
Receivable for sale of property	10,000,000	10,000,000
Deferred tax asset	79,981	57,074
Other loans and advances	7,318	7,318
Receivables total	**10,087,300**	**10,064,392**
Cash	185,166	25,322
Current assets total	**10,272,465**	**10,089,714**
TOTAL ASSETS	**10,272,465**	**10,089,714**

LIABILITIES & EQUITY	This year	Year to date
Debt to mortgage credit institutes	6,109,926	6,109,926

Other long-term liabilities	763,181	800,000
Long-term liabilities total	**6,873,106**	**6,909,926**
Debt to mortgage credit institutes	0	0
Other debt	0	0
VAT	-1,482	-682
Short-term liabilities total	**-1,482**	**-682**
Liabilities total	**6,871,625**	**6,909,244**
Share capital	80,000	80,000
Retained earnings	3,320,841	3,113,067
Proposed dividend	0	0
Equity	**3,400,841**	**3,193,067**
TOTAL LIABILITIES & EQUITY	**10,272,465**	**10,102,310**

Cash flow as of 30-06-2012

	This year	Year to date
Operational cash flows:		
Profit (must match P&L)	-179,180	-386,954
Decrease in trade receivables	-7,966,288	-7,966,288
Decrease in stock	0	0
Decrease in fixed assets	13,621,777	13,621,777
Increase in trade debts	0	0
Increase in taxes owed	-9,793	1,318
Net cash from operational activity	**5,466,515**	**5,269,853**
Financial cash flows:		
Borrowing	845,471	882,291
Investor contribution	-3,692,729	-3,692,729
Dividend paid	-2,098,104	-2,098,104
Net cash from financial activity	**-4,945,362**	**-4,908,542**
Net increase in cash	**521,154**	**361,310**
Initial cash	-335,988	-335,988
Cash (must match balance sheet)	**185,166**	**25,322**

MARTIN MOSFELDT

Income statement as of 30-06-2012

Revenue	0110	0130	0411		
External costs...	0810	0820	0830	0640	1210
...continuation	0610	0831	0611	1220	
Gross Profit					
Personnel Costs	0920	0921	0910		
Depreciation and amortization	1001				
Financial costs	1300				
Profit before tax					
Taxes	1500				
Profit					

Disposition of earnings

Proposed dividends included in own
Reserve for net write-up on equity
Transferred results
Total

Balance sheet as of 30-06-2012

ASSETS
Land and buildings	2410		
Tangible fixed assets, total			
Fixed assets total			
Manufactured goods and	2200		
Total in stock			
Receivable for sale of property	2110	2114	
Deferred tax asset	3120		
Other loans and advances	2120		
Receivables total			
Cash	9001	9002	9003
Current assets total			
TOTAL ASSETS			

LIABILITIES & EQUITY

Debt to mortgage credit institutes	3510
Other long-term liabilities	3520 3522
Long-term liabilities total	
Debt to mortgage credit institutes	3511
Other debt	
VAT	3110 9010 9011
Short-term liabilities total	
Liabilities total	
Share capital	
Retained earnings	1110
Proposed dividend	1803
Equity	
TOTAL LIABILITIES & EQUITY	

Cash flow as of 30-06-2012

Operational cash flows:
Profit (must match P&L)

Decrease in trade receivables	2110 2120 2114 2200 3511
Decrease in stock	
Decrease in fixed assets	2410
Increase in trade debts	
Increase in taxes owed	3110 3120 9010 9011
Net cash from operational activity	

Financial cash flows:

Borrowing	3522 3520 3510
Investor contribution	1110
Dividend paid	1803
Net cash from financial activity	

Net increase in cash

Initial cash	9001
Cash (must match balance sheet)	9002 9003

Chapter Summary

- Cash flow report links P&L earnings to balance sheet cash
- Changes to balance sheet generate an equivalent amount of cash.
- Bookkeeping formula for Cash flow same as P&L
- Accounts allocated to Cash flow same as balance sheet
- Cash flow summation lines calculated bottom-up
- Last line of Cash Flow report has custom format used for assets

6 EXPLANATORY NOTES

Report Lines

The Explanatory Notes could look like this:

	A	B	C
83	**Explanatory notes as of 22-06-2012**		
84		This year	Year to date
85	**External cost**		
86	0810 Services	-8,282	-4,551
87	1220 Insurance	-1,055	-1,055
88	**Total**	**-9,337**	**-5,606**
89			
90	**Taxes**		
91	Last year	3,791	3,791
92	9010 Outgoing VAT		
93	9011 Incoming VAT	-929	-929
94	3110 VAT	509	509
95	**Total**	**3,371**	**3,371**

The starting point for a note is the leftmost column with account numbers, column **A** in the example above. Consider for example the first of the two notes above, "External cost". It's leftmost column is populated with references to the P&L, in this case =A4, =E4 and =F4. These formulas pick out the corresponding texts from the "External cost" report line in the P&L row 4.

I tried more automatic ways of making notes, where the system figured out when another account number was added to some reporting line, and automatically added that account number to the explanatory note. After a while I decided to go with the simpler design explained here.

My inclination towards the simpler design stems from the need for flexibility. There are legal requirements to what notes one must have in one's financial report, and some of the mandatory notes do not lend themselves well to automation. Other stakeholders have unique requirements that are not easily automated either, and therefore, this design in my opinion strikes the right balance between automation, flexibility and simplicity.

Formulas

An explanatory note to a P&L or Cash flow report line starts with the text from that same report line, followed by the accounts that aggregate into that report line. In the External cost note above, consider the "1220 Insurance" line, row 87 in the reports sheet: The amounts shown under "This year" and "Year to date" are calculated with these formulas:

=0.8*SUMIFS(transactions!$E:$E,transactions!$G:$G,$A87)+0.2*SUMIFS(transactions!$E:$E,transactions!$A:$A,"";transactions!$G:$G,$A87)

=0.8*SUMIFS(transactions!$E:$E,transactions!$C:$C,"<"&TODAY(),transactions!$G:$G,$A87)+0.2*SUMIFS(transactions!$E:$E,transactions!$C:$C,"<"&TODAY(),transactions!$A:$A,"",transactions!$G:$G,$A87)

Notice that these are not vector formulas, they do not have curly braces, but otherwise they are the same as the formulas used in the P&L and Cash Flow.

An explanatory note to a balance sheet report line starts with the text from that same report line, followed by a Last year report line, and subsequently followed by the accounts that aggregate into that report line. In the Taxes note above, the values in the Last year report line is calculated as follows:

=$D45

This is because the Taxes report line sits in row 45 of the reports sheet. The rest of a balance sheet explanatory note is the same as a P&L or Cash Flow explanatory note, i.e. for Taxes in row 45, =E45, =F45 and =G45 will pick out the corresponding texts from row 45 in the reports sheet, and the formulas shown above can be copy/pasted to a balance sheet explanatory note too. An asset explanatory note must be formatted like an asset, i.e. with the custom format used for assets, which reverses the sign,

$$-\#.\#\#0;\#.\#\#0$$

A few explanatory notes to the reports listed at the end of the preceding chapter about cash flow are reproduced below. They itemize three report lines from the P&L that a lot of stakeholders would typically find interesting. Notice how the texts are simple copies of the accounts numbers and names from the accounts list. The explanatory note report line that reads "0110 Revenue... " is the result of cells referencing the reports sheet with the formulas =A4, =E4 and =F4.

	A	B	C
73	**Explanatory notes as of 30-06-2012**		
74		This year	Year to date
75	**Revenue**		
76	0110 Revenue from rental	286,383	86,385
77	0130 Agricultural support	14,716	0
78	0411 Profit on sale of land	70,952	70,952
79	**Total**	**372,051**	**157,337**
80			
81	**External costs**		
82	0810 Services	-78,602	-75,402
83	0820 Materials	-19	-19
84	0830 Energy	-51,330	-51,330
85	0640 Land registration fee	-11,555	-11,555
86	1210 Property tax	-19,785	-19,785
87	0610 Attorney assistance	-25,821	-25,821
88	0831 Water	-34,890	-34,890
89	0611 Auditor assistance	-32,000	-32,000
90	1220 Insurance	-19,608	0
91	**Total**	**-273,610**	**-250,802**
92			
93	**Personnel Costs**		
94	0920 Contained withholding tax	-25,692	-25,692
95	0921 Pensions, maternity leave, etc.	-353	-353
96	0910 Salaries paid	-44,308	-44,308
97	**Total**	**-70,353**	**-70,353**

Chapter Summary

- Report lines of explanatory notes are added manually
- Two non-vector bookkeeping formulas for explanatory notes
- Balance sheet notes start with a 'Last year' report line
- Assets notes have custom numeric format for reverse sign

7 GROUPS OF COMPANIES

Adding another Company

To add another company, two new spreadsheets must be defined in the workbook, namely a reports sheet and a transactions sheet, and they can both well be made from some existing company's sheets. In the new transactions sheet, all the bookkeeping records except the automatic accounts must be deleted, and the column with the TRUE/FALSE indicator for checking that active accounts are in fact allocated to report lines must be Find/Replaced to point to the new reports sheet. In the new reports sheet, all the formulas must be Find/Replaced to point to the new transactions sheet. If the workbook contains consolidated reports for multiple companies, those consolidated reports must be updated to include the new company. Finally, any company-specific text in the new reports sheet, the company name for instance, must be modified.

Consolidation from Bookkeeping Records

External as well as internal stakeholders may have a use for special reports, and there may be productivity and work satisfaction to be harvested by providing such custom reports in a timely fashion. If one has several companies, some stakeholders may want consolidated reports rather than individual company reports.

As an example of a consolidated report made directly from bookkeeping records, consider quarterly reporting of VAT. Reporting VAT for all the companies in one go is better, both for reasons of productivity and to ensure consistency across companies.

An example of a consolidated, quarterly VAT report for five companies is shown below:

	Q1		Q2		Q3		Q4	
	I	O	I	O	I	O	I	O
Company 1	-31,962	0	-16,186	0	0	0	-800	0
Company 2	-28,557	230	-64,607	2,247	0	0	-11,000	43,688
Company 3	0	0	0	0	0	0	0	0
Company 4	-509	0	-20	0	0	0	-400	0
Company 5	-118	0	0	0	0	0	-400	0

The formulas that calculate the VAT operate directly on the bookkeeping records of the individual companies. The formula used to calculate Company 1's VAT for the first quarter is:

=0.2*SUMIFS(transactions_company_1!$E:$E,
transactions_company_1!$A:$A,C$2,
transactions_company_1!$C:$C,">31-12-2011",
transactions_company_1!$C:$C,"<1-4-2012")

This formula works for incoming as well as outgoing VAT. The "transactions_company_1" sheet name must be replaced with whatever name one has chosen for the transactions sheets. The formula operates directly on the bookkeeping records of the individual companies, a reflection of the design principle of "no intermediate stored data" explained in the Profit & Loss chapter on page 17. VAT reporting is the kind of thing one does not want to get wrong, because of the risk of planting the company in a far-reaching administrative quagmire. Because this consolidated VAT report operates directly on, and only on, bookkeeping records, one can rest comfortably assured that Excel's flexibility and potential complexity does not befuddle VAT reporting.

Consolidation from Financial Reports

As another example of a consolidated report, consider the liquidity report shown next. This has to be a consolidated report, because the companies are in the same group and can exchange cash freely. There are no SUMIFS involved, the numbers are lifted directly from the financial reports of the individual companies. Notice that group-internal positions must be eliminated for the summation in the group column to be meaningful. An example of this is in the row "Total assets" below, where the groups assets reflect that company 1 owns company 2, 3 and 4.

From the way Excel works and the way this system is designed, it follows that this report is maintained in real time. Whenever some bookkeeping detail is changed, right down to the level of the individual transaction, the report is immediately brought up to date.

		Company			
Year end 2012	Group	1	2	3	4
Sales	562,480	0	372,051	190,429	0
Costs	-308,561	-9,770	-273,610	-15,844	-9,337
Wages	-70,353	0	-70,353	0	0
EBITDA	183,566	-9,770	28,088	174,586	-9,337
Cash Taxes	22,154	2,893	59,727	-43,249	2,784
Cash flow	205,721	-6,878	87,815	13,1336	-6,553
Capital cost	-259,716	-1,800	-254,527	-1,589	-1,800
Cash	524,888	8,923	185,166	252,596	78,204
Total assets	14,307,701	8,201,688	10,272,465	3,945,325	80,988
Total debt	-6,108,798	-2,784	-6,871,625	-42,849	-3,371
Equity	**8,198,904**	**8,198,904**	**3,400,841**	**3,902,476**	**77,617**

An example of a consolidated report where the companies are listed by row is given below. The report uses the operating cash flows from the above report and extrapolates them a few years ahead. In the third year is inserted the terminal value of the companies, i.e. the net future value (their NPV in the future) of their future aggregated cash flows, whereupon their current NPV is calculated.

	Free cash flows			Terminal Value	NPV at 2 %
	2012	2013	2014		
Company 1	-8,678	-6,400	-6,400	-3,877	-24,271
Company 2	-166,712	210,964	215,183	3,890,074	3,835,928
Company 3	129,747	178,629	103,700	3,692,729	3,808,126
Company 4	-8,353	-8,996	-8,996	78,204	46,935
Tax	0	0	0	-35,444	-32,745
Group	**-53,995**	**374,197**	**303,487**	**7,621,686**	**7,633,972**

The formulas behind these reports do not comply with the principle of "no intermediate stored data", because they operate on report lines in the companies' report sheets rather than directly on bookkeeping records. They are however simple arithmetic formulas compared to the SUMIFS that generate report lines, much like control formulas.

To put this non-compliance in perspective, define 'the system' to be the basic bookkeeping and financial reporting system that is implemented in the accounts, transactions and reports sheets. The system must manage large quantities of numbers over time in a robust, predictable and reliable way, and this is achieved by adhering to certain stringent design ideas and principles.

Outside 'the system' one finds the consolidated reports detailed here, which are basically just Excel reports, designed as the user saw fit. Such reports have their place, and I would suggest one should have the necessary non-compliant reports. I would however also suggest, that in order to protect the basic bookkeeping system from complexity, one should not allow non-compliant reports to breed indiscriminately. To exemplify the kind of complexity introduced by consolidated reports, consider the process for adding another company. If the workbook contains consolidated reports for multiple companies, those consolidated reports must be updated to include the new company.

That being said, ad-hoc reports is where Excel excels as a bookkeeping system. Preparing an ad hoc report to support some project is in itself faster within this Excel bookkeeping system, than it would be to extract the data from another system and import into Excel for ad-hoc analysis. The key benefit though is, that the ad-hoc reports are automatically maintained in real time, so one does not have to redo extraction and importing when the preconditions change.

Chapter Summary

- A new company will need two new sheets and two Find/Replace
- A new company may need modifications to consolidated reports
- Consolidated reports can use bookkeeping-type formulas
- Consolidated reports can also use control-type formulas
- Unrestrained reports growth can mess up the bookkeeping system
- Consolidated reports are automatically maintained in real time

8 JOURNAL & LEDGER

One does not need a journal and a ledger to work with the system, because the Data Filtering feature of Excel allows for the rapid extraction and summation of bookkeeping records by account, by document number, by date or indeed by whatever the job at hand necessitates. A printed journal and a printed ledger may be nice to have, nevertheless, just in case. At the end of this chapter is listed a bookkeeping journal and a ledger, seven pages in all, for the financial reports shown in the cash flow chapter on page 27. The silly names in the text fields are chosen to alert the reader, that the dataset is for instructional purposes only.

The journal on the first three pages is a print of the transactions sheet, with field formatting so it will fit the paperback layout. Notice the document field, i.e. the field with the document number that refers to numbers written in blue ink on the documents in the document binders. For the bookkeeping records that are in the future, i.e. the records that belong to the rolling budget, there need not be document numbers.

The ledger on the next four pages is a sorting of the records in the journal on the first three pages by account number and date. Excel has a standard feature that can do this, i.e. sort a copy of the transactions sheet by account number and date. The horizontal lines separating each account are made with conditional formatting to all the fields in the ledger, as follows: Format fields where this formula is true:

=$G1<>$G2

Notice there is no $ in front of the 1 and the 2. The significance of the missing $ is that Excel will insert the actual row number even though the formula reads 1 and 2.

For 25 % VAT, the running tally in the Sum column is calculated as follows:

$$\text{=IF(\$A2="",\$E2,\$E2*0.8)+IF(\$G2=\$G1,\$H1)}$$

Without VAT, the running tally would be

$$\text{=\$E2+IF(\$G2=\$G1,\$H1)}$$

Notice how you can verify the running tally in the ledger against the accounts in the explanatory notes in the chapter of the same name, which begins on page 37. For example, the numbered account 0110 matches the values 286,383 and 86,385 found near the beginning of the ledger.

BOOKKEEPING USING MICROSOFT EXCEL

VAT	Document	Date	Text	Amount	Bank	Account	Allocated
		31.12.12	Automatic	-800.00		9011	TRUE
		02.07.12	Automatic	-48.148.04		9010	TRUE
		31.12.12	Automatic	-127.110.28		9003	TRUE
		02.07.12	Automatic	-58.055.24		9002	TRUE
		01.01.12	Automatic	-335.988.00	B	9001	TRUE
	1	01.01.12	Uncle Scrooge	23.500.00	B	0110	TRUE
I	3	03.01.12	Near By Inc.	-269.00	B	0810	TRUE
I	2	03.01.12	The Free	-1.385.00	B	0810	TRUE
	62	03.01.12	Mrs. Jones	1.45	B	2110	TRUE
	63	03.01.12	Widgets Ltd.	1.998.55	B	2110	TRUE
	64	04.01.12	Whatnots Plc.	10.000.00	B	0110	TRUE
I	6	04.01.12	The Free	3.920.11	B	0820	TRUE
I	8	05.01.12	Mrs. Jones	-7.390.00	B	0831	TRUE
I	9	09.01.12	The Parrot	-3.900.00	B	0830	TRUE
I	10	09.01.12	Uncle Scrooge	-625.00	B	0830	TRUE
I	11	09.01.12	Mr. Smith	-2.550.00	B	0810	TRUE
	65	11.01.12	Widgets Ltd.	1.000.00	B	2110	TRUE
	66	12.01.12	The Parrot	300.000.00	B	3520	TRUE
I	12	12.01.12	Uncle Scrooge	-120.00	B	0810	TRUE
I	13	12.01.12	Near By Inc.	-175.00	B	0810	TRUE
I	7	12.01.12	Mickey Mouse	-20.350.00	B	0810	TRUE
I	14	16.01.12	Mickey Mouse	-3.900.00	B	0830	TRUE
	67	17.01.12	Mickey Mouse	-6.143.00	B	0920	TRUE
I	16	18.01.12	The Parrot	-3.900.00	B	0830	TRUE
	5	20.01.12	Far Away Inc.	-59.66	B	0921	TRUE
	4	20.01.12	Near By Inc.	-68.06	B	0921	TRUE
		20.01.12	The Ugly	2.098.104.00		3522	TRUE
		20.01.12	The Free	-2.098.104.00		1803	TRUE
I	15	25.01.12	The Sad	-24.727.50	B	0810	TRUE
	15	25.01.12	Near By Inc.	-11.555.00	B	0640	TRUE
I	96	26.01.12	Far Away Inc.	11.250.00	B	0110	TRUE
	68	26.01.12	Mrs. Jones	-46.700.00	B	2110	TRUE
	17	30.01.12	Uncle Scrooge	-12.880.00	B	0910	TRUE
	69	31.01.12	Uncle Scrooge	23.500.00	B	0110	TRUE
	70	31.01.12	Whatnots Plc.	2.000.00	B	2110	TRUE
I	23	01.02.12	The Sad	-3.900.00	B	0830	TRUE
I	20	01.02.12	Mrs. Jones	-48.75	B	0820	TRUE
	71	02.02.12	Mrs. Jones	10.000.00	B	0110	TRUE
	72	02.02.12	Uncle Scrooge	31.052.00	B	2110	TRUE
I	21	02.02.12	Near By Inc.	-3.900.00	B	0830	TRUE
	73	02.02.12	The Parrot	1.000.00	B	2110	TRUE
	22	03.02.12	Mr. Smith	14.544.00	B	3110	TRUE
I	24	03.02.12	Whatnots Plc.	-1.312.50	B	0610	TRUE
I	25	06.02.12	Mickey Mouse	-6.993.75	B	0810	TRUE
	17	07.02.12	Far Away Inc.	-90.00	B	0921	TRUE
I	18	07.02.12	Uncle Scrooge	-10.231.55	B	0830	TRUE

	17	07.02.12	Uncle Scrooge	-90.00	B	0921	TRUE
I	26	08.02.12	Whatnots Plc.	-3.900.00	B	0830	TRUE
I	34	09.02.12	The Ugly	-340.00	B	0810	TRUE
	17	10.02.12	Uncle Scrooge	-1.120.00	B	0920	TRUE
	74	13.02.12	Near By Inc.	-2.000.00	B	2110	TRUE
	75	13.02.12	Near By Inc.	1.45	B	2110	TRUE
	76	13.02.12	The Free	2.000.00	B	2110	TRUE
		20.01.12	Far Away Inc.	3.692.729.00		2410	TRUE
		20.01.12	Mickey Mouse	-3.692.729.00		1110	TRUE
	19	22.02.12	The Sad	-19.785.00	B	1210	TRUE
I	27	23.02.12	The Ugly	-7.000.00	B	0830	TRUE
I	32	27.02.12	Uncle Scrooge	-940.00	B	0810	TRUE
	30	29.02.12	Mrs. Jones	-7.857.00	B	0910	TRUE
	77	29.02.12	Mrs. Jones	23.500.00	B	0110	TRUE
	47	29.02.12	The Ugly	19.000.00	B	0110	TRUE
	78	01.03.12	Far Away Inc.	2.000.00	B	2110	TRUE
I	31	02.03.12	Whatnots Plc.	-2.830.00	B	0810	TRUE
I	29	02.03.12	Near By Inc.	-3.895.00	B	0820	TRUE
	79	02.03.12	The Sad	69.979.01	B	3522	TRUE
	30	12.03.12	Mr. Smith	-6.143.00	B	0920	TRUE
	35	12.03.12	Mickey Mouse	-16.000.00	B	0110	TRUE
I	36	14.03.12	The Ugly	-96.00	B	0810	TRUE
	81	19.03.12	Uncle Scrooge	-6.000.00	B	0110	TRUE
	81	19.03.12	Near By Inc.	-3.500.00	B	0110	TRUE
I	33	20.03.12	Near By Inc.	-3.957.30	B	0830	TRUE
I	42	20.03.12	Mr. Smith	-1.000.00	B	0810	TRUE
		20.03.12	Whatnots Plc.	70.952.00		0411	TRUE
		20.03.12	Mrs. Jones	9.929.048.00		2410	TRUE
		20.03.12	The Free	-10.000.000.00		2114	TRUE
		20.03.12	Widgets Ltd.	12.468.00		2200	TRUE
		20.03.12	The Free	-12.468.00		1001	TRUE
		20.03.12	Whatnots Plc.	50.998.55		2110	TRUE
		20.03.12	The Free	-50.998.55		0110	TRUE
	80	21.03.12	Near By Inc.	-9.500.00	B	0110	TRUE
	38	22.03.12	The Parrot	-25.449.38	B	0110	TRUE
	81	26.03.12	The Parrot	9.500.00	B	0110	TRUE
	43	26.03.12	Mrs. Jones	46.700.00	B	2110	TRUE
I	37	29.03.12	Widgets Ltd.	-15.345.31	B	0810	TRUE
	41	30.03.12	The Sad	-7.857.00	B	0910	TRUE
I	34	30.03.12	Whatnots Plc.	-40.000.00	B	0611	TRUE
	58	30.03.12	Near By Inc.	-79.129.08	B	1300	TRUE
	82	30.03.12	The Free	23.500.00	B	0110	TRUE
	83	30.03.12	Mrs. Jones	-600.00	B	1300	TRUE
	84	30.03.12	The Sad	-5.28	B	1300	TRUE
	85	30.03.12	Mickey Mouse	-1.769.26	B	1300	TRUE
I	45	01.04.12	Uncle Scrooge	-1.143.00	B	0810	TRUE
		02.04.12	The Ugly	5.340.000.00		2120	TRUE
		02.04.12	Near By Inc.	-5.340.000.00		3511	TRUE
		02.04.12	Whatnots Plc.	-82.290.57		1300	TRUE
		02.04.12	Uncle Scrooge	82.290.57		3510	TRUE
I	46	02.04.12	The Parrot	-204.00	B	0810	TRUE

BOOKKEEPING USING MICROSOFT EXCEL

	86	02.04.12	The Ugly	2.000.00	B	2110	TRUE
I	39	03.04.12	Widgets Ltd.	-30.963.75	B	0610	TRUE
I	95	03.04.12	Near Bv Inc.	11.250.00	B	0110	TRUE
I	44	04.04.12	Widgets Ltd.	-2.918.75	B	0810	TRUE
	41	10.04.12	The Parrot	-6.143.00	B	0920	TRUE
I	48	10.04.12	Widgets Ltd.	-10.435.00	B	0810	TRUE
	40	13.04.12	Near Bv Inc.	-45.37	B	0921	TRUE
I	52	15.04.12	Far Away Inc.	-1.400.00	B	0810	TRUE
	51	16.04.12	The Parrot	-557.82	B	0831	TRUE
I	87	16.04.12	Mickey Mouse	-1.030.00	B	0810	TRUE
I	54	16.04.12	Mickey Mouse	-35.525.00	B	0831	TRUE
	56	16.04.12	Whatnots Plc.	1.920.879.79	B	2120	TRUE
	88	16.04.12	Mr. Smith	-300.000.00	B	3520	TRUE
	89	16.04.12	Mrs. Jones	-69.979.01	B	3522	TRUE
	53	16.04.12	The Free	-243.53	B	1300	TRUE
	90	16.04.12	The Sad	-2.098.104.00	B	3522	TRUE
	91	16.04.12	The Ugly	800.000.00	B	3522	TRUE
I	50	19.04.12	Mr. Smith	-9.674.75	B	0830	TRUE
I	49	20.04.12	Mrs. Jones	-9.000.00	B	0830	TRUE
I	92	27.04.12	Near Bv Inc.	10.390.00	B	2200	TRUE
	57	30.04.12	Widgets Ltd.	-7.857.00	B	0910	TRUE
	93	30.04.12	Widgets Ltd.	4.000.00	B	0110	TRUE
	94	07.05.12	The Ugly	35.549.00	B	3110	TRUE
	57	10.05.12	Uncle Scrooge	-6.143.00	B	0920	TRUE
I	61	29.05.12	Mrs. Jones	-8.832.01	B	0830	TRUE
I	60	30.05.12	The Free	8.557.61	B	0830	TRUE
	59	31.05.12	Widgets Ltd.	-7.857.00	B	0910	TRUE
	55	31.05.12	Near Bv Inc.	-626.69	B	3110	TRUE
		01.06.12	Whatnots Plc.	33.333.00	B	0110	TRUE
		29.06.12	Uncle Scrooge	-46.630.67	B	1300	TRUE
		01.07.12	Whatnots Plc.	-600.00	B	1300	TRUE
		01.07.12	Far Away Inc.	33.333.00	B	0110	TRUE
		15.07.12	Mickey Mouse	12.596.00	B	3110	TRUE
		01.08.12	Mr. Smith	33.333.00	B	0110	TRUE
		01.08.12	The Parrot	-19.608.09	B	1220	TRUE
		01.09.12	The Free	-42.658.70	B	1300	TRUE
		01.09.12	The Ugly	33.333.00	B	0110	TRUE
		01.10.12	Uncle Scrooge	-600.00	B	1300	TRUE
		01.10.12	The Free	33.333.00	B	0110	TRUE
		01.11.12	The Parrot	33.333.00	B	0110	TRUE
		01.12.12	Mr. Smith	33.333.00	B	0110	TRUE
		31.12.12	Uncle Scrooge	6.175.00	B	0130	TRUE
		31.12.12	Widgets Ltd.	900.00	B	0130	TRUE
		31.12.12	Far Away Inc.	7.641.06	B	0130	TRUE
		31.12.12	Widgets Ltd.	59.726.78		1500	TRUE
		31.12.12	Uncle Scrooge	-59.726.78		3120	TRUE
		31.12.12	Far Away Inc.	36.819.31		3120	TRUE
		31.12.12	Uncle Scrooge	-36.819.31		3522	TRUE
I		31.12.12	The Parrot	-4.000.00	B	0810	TRUE

VAT	Document	Date	Text	Amount	Bank	Account	Sum
	1	1.1.12	The Sad	23,500	B	0110	23,500
	64	4.1.12	Whatnots Plc.	10,000	B	0110	33,500
I	96	26.1.12	Mickey Mouse	11,250	B	0110	42,500
	69	31.1.12	Mickey Mouse	23,500	B	0110	66,000
	71	2.2.12	Widgets Ltd.	10,000	B	0110	76,000
	77	29.2.12	Far Away Inc.	23,500	B	0110	99,500
	47	29.2.12	Whatnots Plc.	19,000	B	0110	118,500
	35	12.3.12	The Ugly	-16,000	B	0110	102,500
	81	19.3.12	Whatnots Plc.	-6,000	B	0110	96,500
	81	19.3.12	Mrs. Jones	-3,500	B	0110	93,000
		20.3.12	The	-50,999		0110	42,001
	80	21.3.12	Uncle Scrooge	-9,500	B	0110	32,501
	38	22.3.12	Near By Inc.	-25,449	B	0110	7,052
	81	26.3.12	The Sad	9,500	B	0110	16,552
	82	30.3.12	The Free	23,500	B	0110	40,052
I	95	3.4.12	The Sad	11,250	B	0110	49,052
	93	30.4.12	Whatnots Plc.	4,000	B	0110	53,052
		1.6.12	Mickey Mouse	33,333	B	0110	86,385
		1.7.12	The Free	33,333	B	0110	119,718
		1.8.12	Mrs. Jones	33,333	B	0110	153,051
		1.9.12	Mrs. Jones	33,333	B	0110	186,384
		1.10.12	The	33,333	B	0110	219,717
		1.11.12	Near By Inc.	33,333	B	0110	253,050
		1.12.12	Mickey Mouse	33,333	B	0110	286,383
		31.12.12	Far Away Inc.	6,175	B	0130	6,175
		31.12.12	Whatnots Plc.	900	B	0130	7,075
		31.12.12	Uncle Scrooge	7,641	B	0130	14,716
		20.3.12	Mickey Mouse	70,952		0411	70,952
I	24	3.2.12	The Sad	-1,313	B	0610	-1,050
I	39	3.4.12	Uncle Scrooge	-30,964	B	0610	-25,821
I	34	30.3.12	Whatnots Plc.	-40,000	B	0611	-32,000
	15	25.1.12	Mr. Smith	-11,555	B	0640	-11,555
I	3	3.1.12	Mr. Smith	-269	B	0810	-215

BOOKKEEPING USING MICROSOFT EXCEL

I	2	3.1.12	Uncle Scrooge	-1,385	B	0810	-1,323
I	11	9.1.12	Mrs. Jones	-2,550	B	0810	-3,363
I	12	12.1.12	Whatnots Plc.	-120	B	0810	-3,459
I	13	12.1.12	Whatnots Plc.	-175	B	0810	-3,599
I	7	12.1.12	The Ugly	-20,350	B	0810	-19,879
I	15	25.1.12	Uncle Scrooge	-24,728	B	0810	-39,661
I	25	6.2.12	Mr. Smith	-6,994	B	0810	-45,256
I	340	9.2.12	The Free	-340	B	0810	-45,528
I	32	27.2.12	Mrs. Jones	-940	B	0810	-46,280
I	31	2.3.12	The Free	-2,830	B	0810	-48,544
I	36	14.3.12	Whatnots Plc.	-96	B	0810	-48,621
I	42	20.3.12	Near By Inc.	-1,000	B	0810	-49,421
I	37	29.3.12	The Free	-15,345	B	0810	-61,697
I	45	1.4.12	Mrs. Jones	-1,143	B	0810	-62,612
I	46	2.4.12	Near By Inc.	-204	B	0810	-62,775
I	44	4.4.12	Whatnots Plc.	-2,919	B	0810	-65,110
I	48	10.4.12	The	-10,435	B	0810	-73,458
I	52	15.4.12	Far Away Inc.	-1,400	B	0810	-74,578
I	87	16.4.12	The	-1,030	B	0810	-75,402
I		31.12.12	Mr. Smith	-4,000	B	0810	-78,602
I	6	4.1.12	Whatnots Plc.	3,920	B	0820	3,136
I	20	1.2.12	Widgets Ltd.	-49	B	0820	3,097
I	29	2.3.12	Uncle Scrooge	-3,895	B	0820	-19
I	9	9.1.12	Mrs. Jones	-3,900	B	0830	-3,120
I	10	9.1.12	Widgets Ltd.	-625	B	0830	-3,620
I	14	16.1.12	The Free	-3,900	B	0830	-6,740
I	16	18.1.12	Mrs. Jones	-3,900	B	0830	-9,860
I	23	1.2.12	Mickey Mouse	-3,900	B	0830	-12,980
I	21	2.2.12	Mr. Smith	-3,900	B	0830	-16,100
I	18	7.2.12	The Ugly	-10,232	B	0830	-24,285
I	26	8.2.12	The Free	-3,900	B	0830	-27,405
I	27	23.2.12	Uncle Scrooge	-7,000	B	0830	-33,005
I	33	20.3.12	Widgets Ltd.	-3,957	B	0830	-36,171
I	50	19.4.12	Far Away Inc.	-9,675	B	0830	-43,911
I	49	20.4.12	The Free	-9,000	B	0830	-51,111
I	61	29.5.12	Near By Inc.	-8,832	B	0830	-58,176
I	60	30.5.12	Mickey Mouse	8,558	B	0830	-51,330
I	8	5.1.12	Far Away Inc.	-7,390	B	0831	-5,912

51	16.4.12	Mr. Smith	-558	B	0831	-6,470
54	16.4.12	Far Away Inc.	-35,525	B	0831	-34,890
17	30.1.12	Near By Inc.	-12,880	B	0910	-12,880
30	29.2.12	The Free	-7,857	B	0910	-20,737
41	30.3.12	Whatnots Plc.	-7,857	B	0910	-28,594
57	30.4.12	The Ugly	-7,857	B	0910	-36,451
59	31.5.12	Near By Inc.	-7,857	B	0910	-44,308
67	17.1.12	Mickey Mouse	-6,143	B	0920	-6,143
17	10.2.12	Mr. Smith	-1,120	B	0920	-7,263
30	12.3.12	The	-6,143	B	0920	-13,406
41	10.4.12	The	-6,143	B	0920	-19,549
57	10.5.12	The Sad	-6,143	B	0920	-25,692
5	20.1.12	The Sad	-60	B	0921	-60
4	20.1.12	Uncle Scrooge	-68	B	0921	-128
17	7.2.12	Mickey Mouse	-90	B	0921	-218
17	7.2.12	Uncle Scrooge	-90	B	0921	-308
40	13.4.12	Whatnots Plc.	-45	B	0921	-353
	20.3.12	The Ugly	-12,468		1001	-12,468
	20.1.12	Uncle Scrooge	-3,692,729		1110	-3,692,729
19	22.2.12	The Free	-19,785	B	1210	-19,785
	1.8.12	Near By Inc.	-19,608	B	1220	-19,608
58	30.3.12	Near By Inc.	-79,129	B	1300	-79,129
83	30.3.12	The Free	-600	B	1300	-79,729
84	30.3.12	Mr. Smith	-5	B	1300	-79,734
85	30.3.12	Mrs. Jones	-1,769	B	1300	-81,504
	2.4.12	Far Away Inc.	-82,291		1300	-163,794
53	16.4.12	Mr. Smith	-244	B	1300	-164,038
	29.6.12	Widgets Ltd.	-46,631	B	1300	-210,668
	1.7.12	The	-600	B	1300	-211,268
	1.9.12	The Sad	-42,659	B	1300	-253,927
	1.10.12	Whatnots Plc.	-600	B	1300	-254,527
	31.12.12	Mrs. Jones	59,727		1500	59,727
	20.1.12	Mickey Mouse	-2,098,104		1803	-2,098,104
62	3.1.12	Near By Inc.	1	B	2110	1
63	3.1.12	The Sad	1,999	B	2110	2,000
65	11.1.12	The	1,000	B	2110	3,000
68	26.1.12	Whatnots Plc.	-46,700	B	2110	-43,700
70	31.1.12	Widgets Ltd.	2,000	B	2110	-41,700

BOOKKEEPING USING MICROSOFT EXCEL

72	2.2.12	The Sad	31,052	B	2110	-10,648
73	2.2.12	The Free	1,000	B	2110	-9,648
74	13.2.12	Mr. Smith	-2,000	B	2110	-11,648
75	13.2.12	Whatnots Plc.	1	B	2110	-11,647
76	13.2.12	The	2,000	B	2110	-9,647
78	1.3.12	Far Away Inc.	2,000	B	2110	-7,647
	20.3.12	Near By Inc.	50,999		2110	43,352
43	26.3.12	Whatnots Plc.	46,700	B	2110	90,052
86	2.4.12	Widgets Ltd.	2,000	B	2110	92,052
	20.3.12	Widgets Ltd.	-		2114	-10,000,000
	2.4.12	The	5,340,000		2120	5,340,000
56	16.4.12	Uncle Scrooge	1,920,880	B	2120	7,260,880
	20.3.12	The Free	12,468		2200	12,468
92	27.4.12	Mr. Smith	10,390	B	2200	20,780
	20.1.12	Mr. Smith	3,692,729		2410	3,692,729
	20.3.12	Widgets Ltd.	9,929,048		2410	13,621,777
22	3.2.12	The Sad	14,544	B	3110	14,544
94	7.5.12	The Free	35,549	B	3110	50,093
55	31.5.12	Near By Inc.	-627	B	3110	49,466
	15.7.12	Uncle Scrooge	12,596	B	3110	62,062
	31.12.12	The Ugly	-59,727		3120	-59,727
	31.12.12	Widgets Ltd.	36,819		3120	-22,907
	2.4.12	Far Away Inc.	82,291		3510	82,291
	2.4.12	The Free	-5,340,000		3511	-5,340,000
66	12.1.12	Uncle Scrooge	300,000	B	3520	300,000
88	16.4.12	Mickey Mouse	-300,000	B	3520	0
	20.1.12	The	2,098,104		3522	2,098,104
79	2.3.12	Far Away Inc.	69,979	B	3522	2,168,083
89	16.4.12	The Sad	-69,979	B	3522	2,098,104
90	16.4.12	Near By Inc.	-2,098,104	B	3522	0
91	16.4.12	Mrs. Jones	800,000	B	3522	800,000
	31.12.12	The	-36,819		3522	763,181
	1.1.12	Automatic	-335,988	B	9001	-335,988
	2.7.12	Automatic	-58,055		9002	-58,055
	31.12.12	Automatic	-127,110		9003	-127,110
	2.7.12	Automatic	-48,148		9010	-48,148
	31.12.12	Automatic	-800		9011	-800

Chapter Summary

- Journal is a copy of the transactions sheet
- Ledger is made by sorting the journal and including a tally
- Journal and ledger is not needed to work with the system...
- ...but may be required or just nice to have nevertheless

9 ERRORS

Conditional Formatting

One class of bookkeeping errors has to do with violation of basic bookkeeping principles. Assets must balance equity and liabilities, debit and credit must balance, and explanatory notes must balance with the report lines they are to explain. To catch this class of errors, checks are put into the financial reports, checks that show up in bright alarming red if there is an error. This is done using Excel's conditional formatting, and the conditional formatting is applied to the report line text in the first column of the financial report, instead of to the numbers that are in error. The way this is done is best explained with an example.

Assume a business has its P&L earnings in row 13 and its Cash Flow earnings in row 58. These should be the same, but only if things are as they should be, i.e. credits are equal to debits and the same accounts are allocated to cash flow as are allocated to the balance sheet. The same conditional formatting applies to both A13 and A58: Format values where this formula is true:

=ABS($B$13-$B$58)+ ABS($C$13-$C$58)>0.001

This makes the report line "Earnings" turn bright red whenever this particular bookkeeping error is active. When it happens, one can go in and check if some newly added balance sheet account has been forgotten in the cash flow, or if perhaps a non-cash VAT transaction has been debited incorrectly.

If the hunt for the errant transaction draws out, one can use Excel copy/paste to speed up the chase – delete some or all the bookkeeping transactions to see if the error goes away, reinsert them with Crtl-z, and keep doing this on smaller and smaller subsets of transactions until the culprit is nailed down.

The same method can be used to make total assets, liabilities and equity turn red if their sum is not zero, or rather, deviates from zero by more than 0.001 currency units. The reason one tests for a near match instead of for an exact match, is because of the inaccuracy inherent in calculations with the computers large but nonetheless limited number of decimals.

To verify explanatory notes, the comparison must be made between the note and the report line. Take for instance the explanatory note mentioned on page 37. It is present in lines 86 to 89 of that reports sheet and has the following formulas:

	A	B	C
86	=A4		
87	=E4	Bookkeeping formulas left out for easier reading	
88	=F4		
89	Total	=SUM(B87:B88)	=SUM(C87:C88)

The conditional formatting to make cells A86 and A89 turn bright alarming red when the note is in error is: Format values where this formula is true:

$$=ABS(\$B\$4-\$B\$89)+ ABS(\$C\$4-\$C\$89)>0.001$$

Using checking-formulas in conditional formatting instead of in cells is smart, because it keeps the cells in the sheets free from checking formulas and thereby simpler, and because it effectively nullifies the risk of checking-formulas spilling over and causing errors in the financial reports.

Control Formulas

Some non-cash transactions are calculated from figures in the financial report. Depreciations for example may be calculated as a percentage of current asset value. Calculating such non-cash transactions by putting formulas directly into the transaction amount in bookkeeping records will not work, because it leads to so-called circular references. The circular reference happens because all the numbers in the financial report are calculated as conditional array sums over all transactions. This means, that even though some particular bookkeeping record has no bearing on the value of some number in the financial report, Excel will still think it has, because the conditional array sum touched that record. Also, because a bookkeeping system is about keeping large quantities of numbers in their right place, there is some merit to maintaining the principle, that the amount in a bookkeeping record must literally be a number instead of something more complicated like a formula.

In the transactions sheet is a separate column with 'control formulas', formulas that calculate depreciation, dividends, debits to match credits and so on. The values in this column are transferred to the bookkeeping. The transfer is done with "copy/paste-special" to paste only the values, not the format or the formula. To verify that control formulas are transferred to bookkeeping records, conditional formatting is used: Format values where this formula is true:

$$=ABS(\$E2-\$I2)>0.001$$

The bookkeeping records amount is in column E, the control formula is in column I, and the absence of a dollar sign after the E and the I makes Excel automatically insert the correct row number. This makes the control field turn alarming red if there is a difference.

I use this facility a lot at the end of the fiscal year, among other things because my companies are jointly taxed with their holding corporation, so that one company's loss may be deducted in another company's gains. The transfer of such a loss to the company that has the gain is balanced by the sale of a so-called tax-asset, and there is a lively traffic of such tax deductions and tax-assets at the time of the annual report. Whenever I change a bookkeeping record, say a deduction, these tax numbers change, and it would be cumbersome and error-prone to recalculate them manually. Conversely, using the control formulas, I can browse through the transactions sheets looking for red, and copy/paste-special the control values into the records until all the red is gone. This takes less than a minute.

Accounting Policies

The International Financial Reporting Standards (IFRSs) are in the process of being adopted worldwide. One of the major drivers of this globalization is, that when an investor in one country buys shares in another, regulatory difficulties arise if accounting practices are incompatible between the two countries. Since the majority of countries desire foreign direct investment, the majority of countries will have to make their accounting practices compatible. China for example, and the US too, are both adopting IFRS, although it will take a while.

The way IFRS standards find their way into a company's bookkeeping is through the accounting policies which is a text contained in the annual report. The company works out its accounting policies, namely a text that describes how it does its bookkeeping. To comply with national law, the company verifies its accounting policies against relevant legal text or commonly accepted practices in that jurisdiction, which in turn is verified against IFRS standards by regulators. For example, if leasing contracts constitute a material part of a company's financing arrangements, that company's accounting policies should devote some words to describing how leasing contracts are accounted for. Those words must comply with law, and will in all certainty comply with what the IFRS has to say about leasing and what is in everybody else's published financial reports too.

It is a bookkeeping error if a particular bookkeeping disposition violates or is not covered by the company's accounting policies. To avoid this error, one should remember to update one's accounting policies whenever some new kind of transaction enters the bookkeeping for the first time. For example, if one enters a leasing arrangement, one should put some words about leasing into the accounting policies, before one attempts to perform the actual bookkeeping.

Accounts Errors

All accounts in the active set must appear at least once in the financial report, in the columns to the right of the report itself, and those accounts that have to do with the balance sheet must appear twice, because they are also used in the cash flow.

To the right of the accounts in the transaction sheet is a column that normally displays "TRUE". If however the accounts are not present in the financial report, it displays "FALSE" in bright, alarming red. The formula to calculate the "TRUE" and "FALSE" is shown here for row number 6:

=COUNTIF(report!$E$3:$Y$53,"="&$G6)>0

The conditional formatting to make it turn red is:

Cell Value = FALSE

One does not need to test separately whether balance sheet accounts are also present in the Cash Flow, because the bookkeeping checks explained in the chapter about bookkeeping errors on page 57 will catch that.

Accounts List Errors

If an active account in the account list has been intentionally or accidentally modified, money will vanish from the financial report because the SUMIFS no longer find a match. The data validation on the account numbers in the transaction sheet ensures that new records contain the updated version of the account, but data validation does not update existing records when accounts are modified.

Such existing records with outdated account information can exist in two places, namely the transactions sheet and the reports sheet. In the transactions sheet they are caught by the conditional formatting of the abovementioned TRUE/FALSE indicator. In the reports sheet, they are caught by the checks mentioned in the previous chapter on bookkeeping errors on page 57.

Accounts Organization

As mentioned in a previous chapter, it is not an error to have unused accounts in the accounts list, but I tidy them up from time to time, if they have become too many. To assist in the tidying up, I have a counter in a column to the right of my accounts list in the accounts sheet, where the number of instances where the account has been used is counted. The formula to do this is shown here for the second row in the accounts sheet:

=COUNTIF(transactions!G:G,A2)

I tend to be quite lenient in the fervor with which I clean up the account list, because there is merit in having a good level of detail in bookkeeping. A simple and effective way to get this detail is to have enough accounts, so it becomes apparent in the explanatory notes what the detailed basis of the report lines are.

Like a lazy tailor sows with a long thread, so it is tempting to bundle all transactions on to just a few accounts, say "0810 Services" for everything from chartered accountants and lawyers to cleaners and masons. A more detailed way to keep the books is to have separate accounts for the four kinds of professional service. Conversely, if one has too many accounts, it increases the likelihood of similar transactions being erroneously charged to different accounts, so tidy accounts is also about verifying this has not happened.

Accounts Numbering

The mechanics of the system does not require accounts to be numbered, but it is good practice to number them nevertheless, in order to have a unique key to reference them by. Also, it is good practice to give similar accounts close numbers. For example one could have all the cost accounts be in the 800 range. To verify that accounts are in fact numbered, conditional formatting can be used to paint unnumbered accounts red in the accounts list. The conditional formatting to do this for four-digit account numbers is:

=NOT(ISNUMBER(VALUE(LEFT($A2;4))))

The topic of accounts numbering in my experience can get quite theoretical, especially in large government organizations, and I have met industry-wide standards for accounts numbering in certain industries too, but there is to the best of my knowledge no universal standard for accounts numbering, neither for their number of digits nor for their values.

Accounts Naming

Unlike the report lines in the financial reports that are defined to a large extent by standards and regulatory requirements, the names of numbered bookkeeping accounts are defined by, oftentimes, the bookkeeper. One reason for this is, that the bookkeeping would stop if the bookkeeper could not name new accounts when necessary.

Consider for example the debts between companies in a group that lends moneys to each other. Obviously, it will be necessary with numbered accounts to keep track of who owes what to whom. Those account names will include the name of the debtor or creditor company, and thus will be too company-specific to adhere to any public standard.

There are in my opinion two requirements one should observe when naming numbered accounts. First, names of employees should not appear in the books directly, because data about people must be kept confidential. Second, the name must be genre-compliant, i.e. the name should sound professional.

An easy-to-read reference publication for the IFRS standard is a publication from 2009 which is available for free for private and non-commercial use from the IFRS website: www.ifrs.org, at least at the time of writing it was. It has the title "International Financial Reporting Standard for Small and Medium-sized Entities (IFRS for SMEs)" with the subtitles "Illustrative Financial Statements" and "Presentation and Disclosure Checklist". Even though one can seldom apply the standard directly because national legislation takes precedence, the standard in its choice of words strikes the right genre and sounds professional. At the time of writing, the IFRS for SMEs was available for free download in Albanian, Armenian, Chinese, Czech, English, French, Hebrew, Italian, Japanese, Kazakh, Macedonian, Mongolian, Polish, Portuguese (Brazil), Romanian, Russian, Spanish and Turkish.

Chapter Summary

- Conditional formatting in reports catches bookkeeping errors
- Control formulas support bookkeeping with calculations
- Conditional formatting checks control formulas vs. bookkeeping
- P&L accounts are allocated once, namely to P&L report lines
- Balance sheet accounts are allocated to Cash Flow report lines too
- Conditional formatting catches accounts allocation errors
- Accounts have numbers and professionally sounding names
- The books should not contain employee names
- Whether bookkeeping is correct is defined in accounting policies
- Accounting policies must honor regulatory requirements
- Global regulation honors IFRS or is in the process of doing so
- IFRS publishes freely downloadable illustrative examples

10 EXERCISES

To see the SUMIFS function, conditional formatting and data validation in action the way they are used in this book, make yourself a new, empty sheet and put the following literal data into it:

	A	B	C	D	E	F	G	H	I	J	K	L
1	Amount	Account	Present	Control	Account list	Report lines	This year	\multicolumn{4}{c}{**Accounts present**}			
2	1				A	Revenue						
3	3				B	Ext. cost						
4	5				C	**Gross profit**						
5	7				D	Salaries						
6	11				E	Depreciation						
7	13				F	**EBIT**						
8	17				G	Fin. earnings						
9	19				H	Fin. costs						
10	23				I	**EBT**						
11	29				J	Tax						
12	31				K	**Earnings**						
13	37											
14	41											
15	43											

To see Data Validation in action, select columns B, H, I, J, K and L and choose "Data Validation", "Allow: List" and "Source: =$D:$D". If you position your cursor in a validated cell, say cell B2, you get a drop-down menu, and if you try to enter something not on the Account list, it won't let you.

To see conditional formatting in action, put the following formula into cell C2 and copy it to the rest of the column:

$$=COUNTIF(\$H\$2:\$L\$12,"="\&\$B2)>0$$

Select the entire column C and choose Conditional Formatting New Formatting Rule Format only cells that contain Cell Value equal to FALSE Format Color red.

You should now see you entire column C taking on the value "TRUE", but as you fill out the fields in column B, they change to "FALSE" in bright alarming red. Fill out the fields in column B as follows:

	A Amount	B Account	C Present	D Control	E Account list	F Report lines	G This year	H I J K L Accounts present
1								
2	1	C	FALSE		A	Revenue		
3	3	B	FALSE		B	Ext. cost		
4	5	A	FALSE		C	**Gross profit**		
5	7	K	FALSE		D	Salaries		
6	11	J	FALSE		E	Depreciation		
7	13	I	FALSE		F	**EBIT**		
8	17	H	FALSE		G	Fin. earnings		
9	19	G	FALSE		H	Fin. costs		
10	23	F	FALSE		I	**EBT**		
11	29	E	FALSE		J	Tax		
12	31	D	FALSE		K	**Earnings**		
13	37	C	FALSE					
14	41	B	FALSE					
15	43	A	FALSE					

BOOKKEEPING USING MICROSOFT EXCEL

To make the red go away and change column C back to "TRUE", fill out columns H to L as follows:

	A	B	C	D	E	F	G	H	I	J	K	L
	Amount	Account	Present	Control	Account list	Report lines	This year	\multicolumn{5}{l}{Accounts present}
1												
2	1	C	TRUE		A	Revenue		A	B			
3	3	B	TRUE		B	Ext. cost		C	D			
4	5	A	TRUE		C	**Gross profit**						
5	7	K	TRUE		D	Salaries		E				
6	11	J	TRUE		E	Depreciation		F				
7	13	I	TRUE		F	**EBIT**						
8	17	H	TRUE		G	Fin. earnings		G				
9	19	G	TRUE		H	Fin. costs		H	I	J		
10	23	F	TRUE		I	**EBT**						
11	29	E	TRUE		J	Tax		K				
12	31	D	TRUE		K	**Earnings**						
13	37	C	TRUE									
14	41	B	TRUE									
15	43	A	TRUE									

To see SUMIFS in action, put the following formula into cell G2 using Ctrl-shift-enter for the curly braces. Copy it to the rest of the column:

$$\{=SUM(SUMIFS(A:A,B:B,H2:L2))\}$$

Delete the formula from the rows that are not used or are intended for summation, i.e. rows 4, 7, 10, 12, 13, 14 and 15. You should see the bookkeeping records being summed up into report lines.

Cell G2 for instance should read 92 because it is the sum of the bookkeeping records in rows 3, 4, 14 and 15. Cell G9 should read 41 because it is the sum of the bookkeeping records in rows 6, 7 and 8.

To complete the example, put the following summation formula in cell G4:

$$=SUM(G2:G3)$$

67

Copy this formula to cells G12. Put the following formula into cell G7:

$$=\text{SUM}(\ G4\text{:}G6)$$

Copy this formula to cell G10. Your sheet should now look like this:

	A	B	C	D	E	F	G	H	I	J	K	L
1	Amount	Account	Present	Control	Account list	Report lines	This year	\multicolumn{4}{c|}{Accounts present}			
2	1	C	TRUE		A	Revenue	92	A	B			
3	3	B	TRUE		B	Ext. cost	69	C	D			
4	5	A	TRUE		C	**Gross profit**	161					
5	7	K	TRUE		D	Salaries	29	E				
6	11	J	TRUE		E	Depreciation	23	F				
7	13	I	TRUE		F	**EBIT**	213					
8	17	H	TRUE		G	Fin. earnings	19	G				
9	19	G	TRUE		H	Fin. costs	41	H	I	J		
10	23	F	TRUE		I	**EBT**	273					
11	29	E	TRUE		J	Tax	7	K				
12	31	D	TRUE		K	**Earnings**	280					
13	37	C	TRUE									
14	41	B	TRUE									
15	43	A	TRUE									

To practice the method for managing calculated bookkeeping records, specify conditional formatting on cell D2: Conditional Formatting New Rule Use a formula to determine which cells to format: Format values where this formula is true

$$=\text{ABS}(\$D2\text{-}\$A2)>0{,}001$$

Choose the color red. Copy the formatting to the rest of column C with Paste-special Formats. Put the following formula in cell D5:

$$=\text{-}G10/3$$

BOOKKEEPING USING MICROSOFT EXCEL

Cell D5 should now show the number -91 in bright alarming red, meaning there is a difference between the bookkeeping record's amount, 7, and its calculated value, -91. To correct this difference, copy cell D5 to cell A5 with Copy/Paste-special Values.

Your sheet should now look like this:

	A	B	C	D	E	F	G	H I J K L
1	Amount	Account	Present	Control	Account list	Report lines	This year	Accounts present
2	1	C	TRUE		A	Revenue	92	A B
3	3	B	TRUE		B	Ext. cost	38	C
4	5	A	TRUE		C	**Gross profit**	130	
5	-91	K	TRUE	-91	D	Salaries	60	E D
6	11	J	TRUE		E	Depreciation	23	F
7	13	I	TRUE		F	**EBIT**	213	
8	17	H	TRUE		G	Fin. earnings	19	G
9	19	G	TRUE		H	Fin. costs	41	H I J
10	23	F	TRUE		I	**EBT**	273	
11	29	E	TRUE		J	Tax	-91	K
12	31	D	TRUE		K	**Earnings**	182	
13	37	C	TRUE					
14	41	B	TRUE					
15	43	A	TRUE					

To practice the method for moving accounts from one report line to another, delete the value in cell I3. You should see cell D5 turn red and change to the value -80.6667, and also cell C12 should become red and change to the value "FALSE".

Put a D into cell I5. The red goes away, and cells C12 and D5 return to their former values. As you can see, you have moved the balance of account "D" from the report line "Ext. cost" to the report line "Salaries". Accordingly, the value of G3 has gone down to 38, the value of G4 has gone down to 130, and the value of G5 has gone up to 60.

To establish the relationship of this exercise to the production system, rename your sheet to "transactions" and make two new sheets named "reports" and "accounts". Cut/paste columns F through L to "reports" and column E to "accounts".

To change the dummy account numbers A, B, C... in to more convincing ones, use "Replace" according to the following table, with the whole workbook as the Replace target, and with tick marks in "Match case" and "Match entire cell contents".

This...	...is replaced with this.
A	1000 Sales
B	1100 Extraordinary income
C	2000 Materials
D	3000 Labor
E	4000 Professional service
F	5000 Depreciation
G	6000 Interest earned
H	7000 Interest due
I	7100 One-time charges
J	7200 Running charges
K	8000 Tax

In the transactions sheet, add the columns "Document", "Date", "Bank" and "VAT". This demonstrates how this exercise links to the production system.

BOOKKEEPING USING MICROSOFT EXCEL

Chapter Summary

- The essentials of the system fit in one 16 x 12 spreadsheet
- The vector SUMIFS can be demonstrated with three arguments
- There is no hard distinction between demo and production

11 TROUBLESHOOTING

Before you apply the methods detailed in this chapter, I strongly suggest you make a back-up copy of your workbook, just in case. One of the techniques applied here is a very general one, sometimes called "variation of parameters". What the method amounts to, is that one changes ones bookkeeping records in a way that sheds light on the trouble. When applying variation of parameters, it must always be understood without saying, that the original records shall be restored once the troubleshooting is finished. This restoration of records is implicitly taken for granted and not explained or detailed in this chapter.

This troubleshooting guide is structured as a series of questions one could ask oneself, followed by a method for answering that question, often by deletion and reinsertion of bookkeeping records. Because the bookkeeping records are in a "flat file" in a workbook spreadsheet, one can delete and reinsert records in seconds by selecting the records in question and pressing the delete key respectively Ctrl-z.

Question: The system does not work at all, why?

Answer: Delete all records except one or two simple bank transactions. You should now see assets, equity and liabilities balancing, P&L and Cash Flow earning identical, and all records "TRUE" as explained in the chapter about errors on page 57.

Question: The system as a whole does not aggregate bookkeeping records correctly, why?

Answer: Delete most records so there is only one record for each account in the active set. Compare the records with the financial report. You should now be able to spot report lines in which the aggregation is faulty.

Question: The aggregation in a specific reporting line is incorrect, why?

Answer: Copy the aggregation formula from a reporting line where the aggregation works as it should. Verify that the formula is entered with curly braces, i.e. with Ctrl-shift-enter. Reenter the accounts in that reporting line's account list to force a rerun of the data validation. If it is an Asset & Liability report line, check that the formula includes last year's balance. If it is an asset account, check that it has the custom format for negative values.

Question: Assets and liabilities do not balance with equity, why?

Answer: Verify that all records show "TRUE" as explained in the chapter about errors on page 57. Check the "equity accounts", i.e. that retained earnings includes this year's earnings. Delete records successively until assets and liabilities do balance equity, thus nailing down the records that cause the problem.

Question: P&L and Cash Flow Earnings do not match, why?

Answer: Check that the Cash Flow report lines all together include all the balance sheet accounts as explained on page 27.

Question: There is a general problem with the VAT, what could it be?

Answer: Check that the data validation on the VAT column in the transactions sheet is active and works the way it should on all records. The VAT formulas depend on that field containing either "", "I" or "O", if the field contains anything else, say the number zero, VAT will not compute correctly.

Question: What does "" mean?

Answer: An empty string.

Question: Assets show up as negative numbers in the balance sheet, why?

Answer: Specify a custom format as explained on page 24. Assets are represented by negative numbers for reasons of mathematical purity.

BOOKKEEPING USING MICROSOFT EXCEL

Theoretical as it sounds, mathematical purity is essential in order to keep the system reliable, predictable, manageable and well-performing.

Question: The drop-down menu with the account list has disappeared from some field, why?

Answer: Probably because cut/paste was used on the field, it cuts the data validation too, use the delete key instead.

Question: The system complains bitterly about a "circular reference" and sets certain fields to zero, why?

Answer: Probably because a control field formula was copied to a bookkeeping record amount field instead of copying its value with Copy/Paste-special. This is explained on page 57.

Question: The year-to-date column in the financial report has incorrect numbers, but the this-year column is okay, why?

Answer: Probably because there is a problem with the date values in the bookkeeping records. These may be downloaded from the Internet bank, and the banks date format may be incompatible with Excel. Replace the incompatible date values with compatible ones.

Question: My cash report line does not match my bank-accounts balance, why?

Answer: Check for duplicate records. When you download this month's bank records from your Internet bank, there may be duplicate records in relation to your rolling budget or last month's records.

Question: My cash report line still does not match my bank-accounts balance, why?

Answer: Check for canceled banking transfers. Some banks leave the canceled transfers in the download with a special marker that has no equivalent in this system.

Question: I need to check my bank-account transactions one-at-a-time, but my transactions sheet has them intermixed with non-banking transactions. How do I extract a pure bank-account transaction summary?

Answer: Specify Data filtering on the "Bank" column (the column with the "B"s in the transaction sheet).

Question: I need to go through all transactions involving vendor so-and-so. How do I extract the relevant transactions?

Answer: Specify Data filtering on the descriptive text of the bookkeeping records. The resulting drop-down list will display the various formats which that vendors name has been entered with, for you to tick off.

Question: I have one account loaded with too many different kinds of cost and need to split it up on several accounts. How do I do this smartly?

Answer: Use Data filtering on the account number to pick out the relevant records. Select the records that need changing and use Find/Replace to change their accounts.

Question: I have an explanatory note where the sum total does not compute. Why could that be?

Answer: Probably the report line the note relates to has been allocated some more accounts, but the note itself has not been expanded accordingly. Expand the note by adding the missing accounts from the report lines account sub-list.

Question: The account sub-list to the right of the reporting lines in my financial report are not readable because they won't fit the display window. What can I do?

Answer: The accounts adhere to a number-text layout also to address the issue of maintaining readability when display space is limited. Format the account fields without Text wrap and positioned to the left, and make the fields four characters wide (assuming you use four digits for account numbers). This will display the account list as an intelligible horizontal list of four digit numbers.

Question: My system responds sluggishly yet does not appear defective. Why could that be?

Answer: The formulas all use entire column array notation, e.g. A:A. This is smart because it places no hard limits on how many records and accounts the system can handle, but it has a performance drawback. If a lot of empty records, say 10000, are added to one of the sheets, Excel will painstakingly work its way through them, thinking they might contain data. You can see whether this is the case by looking at the slider to the right of the sheet. If the slider is very small, it means the sheet is very big. Remove the empty records.

Question: I will have several companies in my workbook. Are there any good ideas with respect to naming the sheets?

Answer: Sheet naming like so much else in Excel is not binding, because when one changes a sheet name on the fly, Excel will update references to that sheet name dynamically and automatically. Personally I like to use two letter company identifiers with a single letter type identifier, to give me short, handy three letter names for my sheets. Company "xx" for instance will have sheets "xxr" and "xxt" for reports and transactions.

Question: My accountant says he or she does not agree with using negative numbers for accounting assets. How can I answer this?

Answer: The chapter about cash flow on page 27 is written with considerable redundancy and many very detailed examples that explains the use of negative numbers for assets. For academic support for the idea of distinguishing accounting assets and accounting liabilities by their sign only, look to corporate finance, where the term 'asset' applies to both debts and receivables, and the term 'liability' is not used.

Chapter Summary

- Variation of parameters is a powerful troubleshooting method...
- ...but one should always take a backup before beginning
- This chapter contains assorted uncategorized tips and tricks

12 QUICK REFERENCE

This space intentionally left blank

Columns used in spreadsheets

Column	Transactions	Reports	Accounts
A	VAT	Report lines	Account number- and name
B	Document	This year	Active count
C	Date	Year to date	
D	Text	Last year	
E	Amount		
F	Bank		
G	Account		
H	Allocated		
I	Control		
J		Accounts sub-list	
.			
.			
.			
X			
Y			

Bookkeeping formulas without VAT and row number set equal to 7

	This year	Year to date
P&L	{=SUM(SUMIFS(transactions!$E:$E,transactions!$G:$G,$E7:$Y7))}	{=SUM(SUMIFS(transactions!$E:$E,transactions!$E:$E,"<"&TODAY(),transactions!$G:$G,$E7:$Y7))}
Balance sheet	{=$D7+SUM(SUMIFS(transactions!$E:$E,transactions!$G:$G,$E7:$Y7))}	{=$D7+SUM(SUMIFS(transactions!$E:$E,transactions!$E:$E,"<"&TODAY(),transactions!$G:$G,$E7:$Y7))}
Cash flow	{=SUM(SUMIFS(transactions!$E:$E,transactions!$G:$G,$E7:$Y7))}	{=SUM(SUMIFS(transactions!$E:$E,transactions!$E:$E,"<"&TODAY(),transactions!$G:$G,$E7:$Y7))}
Explanatory notes	=SUMIFS(transactions!$E:$E,transactions!$G:$G,$A7)	=SUMIFS(transactions!$E:$E,transactions!$C:$C,"<"&TODAY(),transactions!$G:$G,$A7)

BOOKKEEPING USING MICROSOFT EXCEL

Bookkeeping formulas with VAT and row number set equal to 7

	This year	Year to date
P&L	{=SUM(0.8*SUMIFS(transactions!$E:$E,transactions!$G:$G,$E7:$Y7)+0.2*SUMIFS(transactions!$E:$E,transactions!$A:$A,"",transactions!$G:$G,$E7:$Y7))}	{=SUM(0.8*SUMIFS(transactions!$E:$E,transactions!$E:$E,"<"&TODAY(),transactions!$G:$G,$E7:$Y7)+0.2*SUMIFS(transactions!$E:$E,transactions!$C:$C,"<"&TODAY(),transactions!$A:$A,"",transactions!$G:$G,$E7:$Y7))}
Balance sheet	{=$D7+SUM(0.8*SUMIFS(transactions!$E:$E,transactions!$G:$G,$E7:$Y7)+0.2*SUMIFS(transactions!$E:$E,transactions!$A:$A,"",transactions!$G:$G,$E7:$Y7))}	{=$D7+SUM(0.8*SUMIFS(transactions!$E:$E,transactions!$E:$E,"<"&TODAY(),transactions!$G:$G,$E7:$Y7)+0.2*SUMIFS(transactions!$E:$E,transactions!$C:$C,"<"&TODAY(),transactions!$A:$A,"",transactions!$G:$G,$E7:$Y7))}
Cash flow	{=SUM(0.8*SUMIFS(transactions!$E:$E,transactions!$G:$G,$E7:$Y7)+0.2*SUMIFS(transactions!$E:$E,transactions!$A:$A,"",transactions!$G:$G,$E7:$Y7))}	{=SUM(0.8*SUMIFS(transactions!$E:$E,transactions!$E:$E,"<"&TODAY(),transactions!$G:$G,$E7:$Y7)+0.2*SUMIFS(transactions!$E:$E,transactions!$C:$C,"<"&TODAY(),transactions!$A:$A,"",transactions!$G:$G,$E7:$Y7))}
Explanatory notes	=0.8*SUMIFS(transactions!$E:$E,transactions!$G:$G,$A7)+0.2*SUMIFS(transactions!$E:$E,transactions!$A:$A;"";transactions!$G:$G,$A7)	=0.8*SUMIFS(transactions!$E:$E,transactions!$C:$C,"<"&TODAY(),transactions!$G:$G,$A7)+0.2*SUMIFS(transactions!$E:$E,transactions!$C:$C,"<"&TODAY(),transactions!$A:$A,"",transactions!$G:$G,$A7)

INDEX

account aggregation, 5
accounting, 10
accounting policies, 57, 58, 61
accounting practices, 57
accounting rules, 13
accounts, 4, 5, 6, 7, 10, 11, 12, 14, 18, 22, 23, 24, 25, 26, 27, 36, 37, 39, 42, 46, 55, 58, 59, 60, 61, 67, 72, 73, 74
accounts list, 11, 23, 59
accounts naming, 60
accounts numbering, 59
accounts organization, 59
accounts sheet, 6, 7
active set, 23, 26, 58, 72
adding another company, 39
addressing people, 3
ad-hoc reports, 42
advanced use of SUMIFS, 5
advantages, 11
aggregated cash flows, 41
alarm, 7
Albanian, 60
amount, 9
annual report, 15, 16, 22, 57
arithmetic formulas, 41
arithmetic operators, 7
Armenian, 60
array notation, 11, 18, 74
asset, 13, 22, 37, 56, 57, 72
Assets, 12, 14, 38, 55, 72
auditing, 10
authorities, 15, 16, 22
automatic account, 11, 12, 13
automatic accounts, 11, 12, 22, 25
balance sheet, 13, 21, 23, 24, 25, 26, 27, 31, 33, 34, 36, 55, 58, 72

bank, 9
bank balance, 9
bank interface, 9
bank statement, 4
bank transactions, 11
basic bookkeeping principles, 55
bidirectional relationship, 6
bills, 10
binders, 10, 19, 45
blue ink, 10, 45
board, 16
bookkeeper, 60
bookkeeping, 9
bookkeeping disposition, 58
bookkeeping errors, 13, 59
bookkeeping formulas, 7
bookkeeping records, 5
Brazil, 60
budget cuts, 17
budget variation, 16, 17
Cash at end of year, 25, 26
cash flow, v, 5, 7, 25, 26, 27, 34, 36, 55, 58, 61, 71, 72, 75
cash flow from financing, 26
cash flow from operations, 26
cash reserves, 17
chapter Summary, 8, 14, 20, 24, 34, 38, 43, 54, 61, 69, 76
chartered accountants, 59
check, 55, 72, 73
checks, 55, 58, 59, 61
checks and balances, 7
China, 57
Chinese, 60
circular references, 56
cleaners, 59
close numbers, 59
color, 7
columns,, 10

comma, 3
comma-separated file, 9
commonly accepted practices, 58
companies in a group, 60
company credit card, 10
complexity, 5, 10
conditional array sums, 56
conditional formatting, 4, 7, 8, 45, 55, 56, 57, 58, 59, 61, 63, 64, 66
consistency across companies, 39
consolidated, 17, 39, 40, 41, 42
consolidation, 39, 40
consolidation from bookkeeping records, 39
consolidation from financial reports, 40
control formulas, 6, 7, 41, 56, 57, 61
control-type formulas, 43
copy/paste, 11
copy/paste-special, 57
cost, 13, 15, 23, 35, 36, 63, 64, 65, 66, 67, 74
cost accounts, 59
countries, 57
credit, 10, 13, 55
creditor, 60
credits, 55, 57
critical success factor, 5
ctrl-shift-enter, 3
Ctrl-shift-enter, 18, 65, 72
currency units, 22, 56
current NPV, 41
current transactions, 16
custom format, 22, 26, 37, 72
custom reports, 39
customization of report lines, 5
Czech, 60
dashes, 9

data about people, 60
data entry, 7
data filtering, 23, 45
data validation, 4, 7, 11, 18, 59, 63, 72, 73
data Validation, 11, 64
database, 5
date, 9
debit, 13, 55
debits, 55, 57
debtor, 60
debts, 21, 31, 33, 60, 75
decimal mark, 3
deduction, 57
depreciation, 7, 13, 57
depreciations, 56
descriptive text, 9
design, 4, 5, 17, 18, 22, 36, 40, 42
design victory, 5
detailed basis, 59
development, 4
dividends, 29, 30, 32, 33, 57
document numbers, 10, 45
dot-decimal format, 9
dots, 9
double-entry bookkeeping, 13
download, 9
dropdown menu, 11
drop-down menu, 7
drop-down menu, 11
drop-down menu, 64
drop-down menu, 73
earnings, 15, 21, 22, 26, 55, 63, 64, 65, 66, 67, 72
employee names, 61
employees, 60
empty cell, 11
English, 3, 60

equity, 12, 21, 22, 27, 30, 32, 55, 56, 71, 72
error, 55, 56, 57, 58, 59
errors, 4
exact match, 56
Excel, i, 3, 4, 7, 9, 11, 12, 13, 17, 18, 19, 22, 23, 40, 42, 45, 55, 56, 57, 73, 74, 75
expected income, 16
experiment, 19
explanatory note, 36, 37, 56, 74
explanatory notes, 16, 37, 38, 46, 55, 56, 59
external costs, 16
extract, 42, 73, 74
financial dilemma, 16, 17
financial dilemmas, 16
financial projections, 16
financial report, 5, 22, 23, 36, 55, 56, 58, 72, 73, 74
financing arrangements, 58
Find/Replace, 9, 23, 43, 74
Find/Replace function, 9
fiscal year, 12, 16, 57
fixed budget, 16
flat file, 5, 71
foreign direct investment, 57
formalities, 3
four-digit account numbers, 59
freeze the top lines of a sheet, 12
French, 60
function calls, 5
future transactions, 16
gender, 3
genre, 60
getting started, 3
global regulation, 61
globalization, 57
good practice, 59
group column, 40
group of companies, 17
group-internal positions, 40
hard limit, 11, 18
Hebrew, 60
hiring freezes, 17
housekeeping, 23, 27
human factor, 19
ICT system, 5
IFRS, 15, 57, 60
IFRS for SMEs, 15, 60
ignore blank, 11
illustration, 6
Illustrative Financial Statements, 15, 60
import, 42
inaccuracy, 56
in-cell dropdown, 11
incoming VAT, 11
initial bank account balance, 12
intermediate stored data, 17, 40, 41
International Financial Reporting Standards, 57
Internet, 9, 15, 73
internet bank, 9
investment stops, 17
investors, 16
Italian, 60
Japanese, 60
journal, 5, 13, 45, 54
jurisdiction, 58
Kazakh, 60
language, 3
language conventions, 3
lawyers, 59
leasing contract, 58
leasing contracts, 58
ledger, 13, 45, 46, 54
level of detail, 59

liabilities, 12, 22, 26, 27, 31, 33, 55, 56, 71, 72, 75
limiting factor, 19
liquidity report, 40
list of accounts, 7
literal data, 63
local sales tax, 4
locales, 3
loss, 22, 57
Macedonian, 60
magic, 27
maintenance, 7
masons, 59
master, 6
Match case, 23, 68
Match entire cell contents, 23, 68
material part, 58
mathematical purity, 22, 27, 72
matrix, 18
mistyped accounts, 11
money, iii, 23, 58
Mongolian, 60
motivation, 4
multi-operand function calls, 3
national law, 58
national legislation, 60
near match, 56
negative numbers, 22, 26, 27, 72, 75
negative sign, 12
net future value, 41
non-banking transactions, 13
non-cash transactions, 56
non-compliant reports, 42
NPV, 41
operating cash flows, 41
outdated account information, 59
outgoing VAT, 11
P&L, 13, 15, 16, 17, 18, 22, 23, 26, 35, 36, 55, 71, 72

performance, 19, 74
permitted values, 7
Polish, 60
Portuguese, 60
preconditions change, 42
Presentation and Disclosure Checklist, 60
printed journal, 45
printed ledger, 45
productivity, 39
professional service, 59, 87
programming, 7
published financial reports, 58
quarterly reporting, 39
real time, 40, 42, 43
receivable interest, 16
red, 7
reference model, 5
reference publication, 60
regulatory difficulties, 57
regulatory requirements, 60, 61
Replace Options, 23
report lines, 4, 5, 6, 7, 15, 18, 22, 26, 41, 55, 59, 60, 65, 72, 74
reports, 5
reports sheet, 6, 36, 37, 39, 56, 59
requirements, 4
resolve, 4
retained earnings, 22, 72
risk, 4
rolling budget, 16, 45, 73
Romanian, 60
running tally, 46
Russian, 60
sales projections, 16
sales tax, 4
semicolon, 3
several companies, 39, 75
similar accounts, 59

Small and Medium-sized Entities, 15, 60
solutions, 4
sorting, 13, 45, 54
Spanish, 60
special reports, 39
spreadsheet, 9, 13, 18, 22, 71
spreadsheets, 5
stakeholder, 16
stakeholders, 4, 36, 37, 39
standardization, 15
standards for accounts numbering, 60
stateless, 17
structure, 5
sub-list of accounts, 5
such tax deductions, 57
SUM, 5, 7, 16, 17, 18, 22, 23, 27, 56, 65, 66, 78, 79
SUMIFS, 3, 5, 7, 12, 17, 18, 22, 27, 36, 40, 41, 59, 63, 65, 78, 79
system, 3
tax-assets, 57
terminal value, 41
transaction, 9
transaction sheet, 6, 23, 58, 59, 74
transactions, 5
transactions sheet, 6, 11, 19, 39, 45, 54, 57, 59, 68, 72, 73
troubleshooting, 19, 71
Turkish, 60
unidirectional relationship, 6
unique key, 59
unrestrained reports growth, 43
US, 16, 57
Value Added Tax, 4, 11
variation of parameters, 71
VAT, 4, 8, 11, 12, 13, 14, 18, 25, 26, 27, 29, 31, 33, 35, 39, 40, 46, 47, 50, 55, 68, 72, 78, 79
VBA coding, 7
vector formula, 18
vector SUMIFS, 69
verification, 10
web bank, 9
what-if calculations, 19
work satisfaction, 39
workbook, 5, 19, 23, 39, 42, 68, 71, 75
www.ifrs.org, 60
XML, 9

ABOUT THE AUTHOR

Martin Mosfeldt is a Danish national and lives in Denmark on his country estate an hour west of Copenhagen. His CV is published separately on the World Wide Web. Some headlines:

- 1955 born in Denmark
- 1978 Master of Science in Engineering
- 1986 Advisory System Engineer, IBM
- 2001 Product Manager, Intel
- 2010 Master of Business Administration (Henley)

He has ten years of cross-industry management consulting experience obtained in small ICT oriented professional service firms. Since 2010 he has seen himself as a general businessman with no affinity for any one particular industry over another.

Printed in Great Britain
by Amazon